Out of Whole Cloth

Out of Whole Cloth

The Life of Bettye Kimbrell

by
Joyce H. Cauthen

Library of Congress Control Number: 2013912601

ISBN-13: 978-1490546186
ISBN-10: 1490546189

Contents

Illustrations

Out of Whole Cloth

Introduction

Whole cloth? I first heard this term from Bettye Kimbrell, the exquisite quilter who is about to tell you her story. To Bettye a whole-cloth quilt is one whose top is made from an entire piece of fabric rather than from scraps and patches. Such quilts, usually single pieces of white or unbleached fabric decorated only with stitches, suggest to me human qualities like strength, honesty, integrity, and straightforwardness. There are no flashy colors, just designs, subtly elaborate, created by needle and thread on a base of solid fabric.

I can think of no better way to describe Bettye Kimbrell than to say she is cut out of whole cloth. For the many years I have been working on this book I have wanted to use the phrase as its title. When I researched it, however, I was dismayed to learn that in the mid-nineteenth century the term had taken on a very different meaning from what I had in mind. The first definition of "whole cloth" listed in most dictionaries is "fictitious, untrue, improvised, or fabricated," with examples such as "These incidents were manufactured out of whole cloth; they never occurred." I reluctantly gave up on using the phrase as a title, but continued to think about it. Over time I realized that in one way the negative definition correlated with Bettye's story. She had to fabricate a good life for her family. A motherless child, then a child bride with few good role models and little education, Bettye had to figure out on her own how to create a safe, loving environment for her five children and find satisfaction for herself. In this book she tells us how she did it. As you can see, I have decided to reject the definition of "whole cloth" as "made-up" and use it as the title of an absolutely true story.

The idea for this book came into being as Bettye Kimbrell and I drove from Birmingham to Montgomery and back many times in the 1990s. We were working on a series of Alabama Folklife Festivals being held in both of those cities. I directed the festivals and Bettye exhibited her quilts at them and helped in any way she could, such as ironing and folding a hundred festival T-shirts that arrived at the last minute too wrinkled to sell. The trip to planning meetings was one and a half hours each way, but Bettye's stories of her childhood in rural West Alabama in the 1940s made the time fly. I savored them, finding them nostalgic and pastoral, until I heard her say that when she was eight years old her mother left Bettye's father and their five children for another man. To make it worse, she remained with him in the little town where her abandoned family lived.

Bettye was no longer talking about the good old days. As a child of the 1950s I well remember the stigma attached to divorce—even to the children of divorce. No child wants to be different. In those times when divorce was uncommon, children in single-parent homes felt very different from their schoolmates. I wondered how Bettye was affected by her mother's scandalous behavior and eventually asked her if I could interview her for a possible book. The answer obviously was yes. Bettye had a store of knowledge and wisdom growing out of her experience that she was eager to share. We began our interviews on March 11, 1996, with a tape recorder sitting on the kitchen table in her Mt. Olive, Alabama, home. By the time we finished, I possessed a drawer full of cassette tapes and a folder full of digital recordings on my computer, all capturing the voice of Bettye Kimbrell as she recalled the details of her life.

Out of Whole Cloth is told in Bettye's own words with two exceptions. First, I wrote passages, when needed, to tie groups of experiences into thematic chapters and to serve as transitions between different periods in her life. Second, all five of her children, her brother Milford, her aunt Ezzie, and a group of her Kimbrell in-laws granted me interviews that were rich in detail and filled with enviable word choices. Keeping the story "whole cloth," I did not want to have a patchwork of voices telling it, but I could not resist helping myself to some of their on-the-mark expressions. So I let Bettye say them. You can recognize such borrowings, as they usually follow phrases like "Cindy says," or "Scott remembers."

Bettye's recall of detail makes her a wonderful person to interview and her story a fascinating one to read. It also makes forgiveness difficult for her. I regret any embarrassment this book may cause those she remembers unfavorably. Readers will understand, I hope, that these kinfolks lived in the same harsh conditions as Bettye and found their own ways to deal with them.

I sincerely appreciate the help of Bettye's family members in my research for this book. Some experiences were hard for them to talk about and tears were shed in most of the interviews, but no one said "Don't write about that." They all agree that the story of their mother and father is worth telling. I especially appreciate the hours Cindy Kimbrell Denton put in to creating the wonderful cover and interior of *Out of Whole Cloth*. Now, in 2013, after years of interviews, telephone calls, and one long break while this writer was otherwise occupied, we have finished our book about hurdles overcome, a husband loved, children raised, and quilts with thousands of tiny stitches.

—Joyce H. Cauthen

Acknowledgements

In addition to the Kimbrell family, I would like to thank the much smaller Cauthen family for their contributions to this book. My husband Jim has helped in innumerable ways, the most important being the enthusiasm and support he had for the project throughout the 17 years I sporadically worked on it. My daughter, Carey Cauthen, helped me do archival research for my first book on fiddle music when she was nine years old. Now a professional editor and website designer, her contributions to this book have been invaluable.

Another family helped give Bettye's story a happy ending—the family of American folklorists, past and present, who founded and sustained agencies that have honored her. Among these is Archie Green (1917-2009) who believed that our government should support the study and preservation of expressions of our nation's folk culture. He lobbied tirelessly for the passage of the 1976 American Folklife Preservation Act that funded the American Folklife Center, a division of the Library of Congress. There is Bess Lomax Hawes (1921-2009) who as director of the Folk and Traditional Arts program of the National Endowment for the Arts created the National Heritage Fellowships and encouraged the establishment of folklife programs in each state. Her successor, Barry Bergey, has kept these programs strong. Alabama's folklife program has had the great fortune of being an agency of the Alabama State Council on the Arts (ASCA), directed by Al Head, a tremendous supporter of the state's folk arts. ASCA's Folklife Program and its related division, the Alabama Center for Traditional Culture, staffed by Joey Brackner, Anne Kimzey, Steve Grauberger, and Deborah Boykin, creates publications, produces radio shows, assists with television documentaries, administers an apprenticeship program and does whatever else it can to assure that Alabamians recognize and appreciate their traditional potters, musicians, quilters, storytellers, farmers, herbalists, cooks, and their own community's folkways. ASCA also provides financial support and staff expertise to the Alabama Folkife Association, an independent non-profit organization that sponsors fieldwork and programs about the state's folk traditions. Each of these agencies played a part in Bettye Kimbrell's success and helped her carry out her mission of teaching others about hand quilting. She would have quilted continuously and beautifully without them. However, without them few of us would have had the opportunity to enjoy her quilts and hear her story.

Map of Central West Alabama

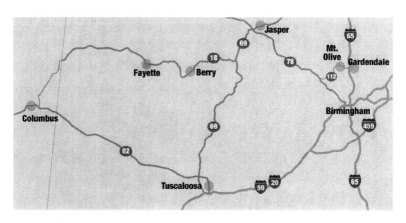

Except for six months in Chicago, I have mostly been in Berry or Mt. Olive or on the road between them.

The only time I was ever in Mississippi was the day Calvin and I went to Columbus to get married. Calvin had on his newest khaki shirt and work pants and I was wearing a blue taffeta dress with a circle-tail skirt. I was thirteen years old and Calvin was seventeen. I'm sure that judge looked at us after the vows and thought, "What did I just do?" He didn't know it was going to take.

I was born on November 22, 1936, in west Alabama, about halfway between Berry and Fayette. My memories begin when I was six or seven years old and we were living on Melvin Pinion's place below Berry. Daddy was working at a sawmill and Mother did seasonal work in the field for the Pinions.

My mother, Pearl Whitson, was an attractive woman, shorter and smaller boned than I am. She always had a nice hairdo that she cut herself and she could see a dress she liked in a magazine and make it. She was a good gardener, too, and could grow vegetables out of flint rock. She never seemed satisfied with life, though. She had lost her own mother when she was a child and moved in with the Sextons, her older sister's family, after her father married a woman she couldn't get along with. The Sextons were better off than most folks around there; at least they owned enough land that they could rent some out to share croppers who paid them half of what they earned from their crops each year. Mother had trouble getting along with the Sextons, too, and things came to a head over religion. They had been Methodists at Oak Grove until they joined the Holiness church and got real intense with their religion. They started saying grace before meals and praying at bedtime and expected her to get down on her knees and do the same. But she refused and her sister undertook to make her. During all the turmoil that followed she met a nice-looking young man whose family was sharecropping on the Sexton's land. So when Mother was sixteen she married Bradley Whitson and moved in with his family.

My daddy was a lean man of medium height and gentle disposition. When I watch old Henry Fonda movies, I realize how much my father looked and talked like him. He was intelligent and though he didn't finish high school he was the only one of the three brothers who could help his sisters with their homework. He could fix anything that was broken. He might have to make a part to do it, but he had the ability to make that part. Lumber was the big industry in our part of the country. Because he was a master at sharpening saws and fixing broken-down mills, he could always get a job at one of the lumber companies. He also had the ability to look at a load of logs on a truck and tell how many board feet of lumber it held. He could count up lumber in his head faster than they can do it with a computer now. And he was a first-class gunsmith. Out in the country there weren't any repair shops and if you could do something well, folks came to you for help. People were always bringing Daddy guns to fix. With all of his talent, Bradley Whitson could have been a man of means but he lacked ambition and seemed content to take the easiest path through life. I truly believe that if he had met the right woman, one who would be a helpmate to him, we all would have had better lives, but it didn't happen that way.

Mother and Daddy's first child, Geraldine, died when she was a few months old. Today people would say that she died of sudden infant death syndrome but Daddy's family said that she died of boll hives. They believed that most babies break out in hives at some point. If a baby with hives gets chilled, the hives will go in on it—that's how they said it—go in on the baby, wrap around its heart or lungs and kill it. The family and neighbors thought that maybe Mother had been careless in bathing the baby. She probably carried around a big load of guilt because of Geraldine's death.

I'm the oldest of the surviving children. At the time we lived on the Pinion place there were three children besides me. My sister Esta was two years below me, my brother Karrold was two years below her and there was a brand new baby brother, Milford. We lived in an old country house with a high-pitched shingle roof and small front porch. In the morning Daddy would go off to work at the sawmill in Berry and Mother would take us in a wagon to work in the bottoms next to the creek a couple of miles away from the house. We would take a gallon of buttermilk, a pan of cornbread that she had made that morning, and cups to eat it out of for lunch. The buttermilk would stay cold in the creek until it was time to eat.

Even at that point we had our own cow, Peggy. Mother milked—everybody did. If you had children to feed you had to have milk and butter and raise your own chickens and grow whatever vegetables you could, because there was no Piggly Wiggly on the corner. Mother had a garden and she canned and dried her vegetables and fruit to get us through the winter. Later on she shirked her responsibilities, but she was a talented woman and in those early years she worked hard.

Before we moved to Berry and Mother left us, our life was nothing out of the ordinary. We got our water from a spring; we heated with a fireplace and cooked on a wood stove. The house wasn't sealed; the inside walls were just the back side of the outside walls. In the winter everything in it would freeze at night and there wasn't a thing to do about it except wear a lot of clothes and sleep under a pile of quilts. The boys wore long-handle underwear and we girls wore undershirts and underpants down to our knees, heavy stockings on our feet and clodhopper shoes to keep us warm. It wasn't just us; everyone we knew had a cold house. We were dirt-poor farmers but everybody else and his brother was, too.

As the eldest, I had to watch out after Esta and Karrold and keep Milford on the pallet while Mother worked in the cotton and corn. I was about six years old and at times got distracted by something silly that Esta and Karrold were doing. Once I let Milford get into an ant bed and I got my behind whipped for it. That was about the time that we got Butch, a puppy who soon took over my job. His mother was a pretty collie-looking dog that Daddy shot because she was killing a neighbor's chickens. Most country people have no qualms about shooting dogs that aren't wanted, and I guess Daddy saw no reason his six-year-old daughter shouldn't help him carry off her remains. I couldn't eat for a week after that. Every time I'd try to eat, I'd think about that dead dog. But we got to keep Butch who grew up with us and constantly watched over us.

In the middle years of World War II the sawmills were prospering and Daddy was making good money, so he decided to move us to Berry, 12 miles away. That was in the springtime of 1943, right after I finished first grade. Daddy rented a house just a block away from the sawmill. It had electric lights and sealed interior walls. He bought my mother a living room suite with a sofa, chairs and end tables, and a bedroom suite. We had never seen anything like that. Poor country people usually just had a kitchen table, some straight chairs, and a few beds, so we felt ourselves to be quite fine despite the fact that we still cooked on a wood-burning stove, used an outdoor privy, and got our water from a well that we shared with a neighbor. The really big difference was that Berry had stores and we could walk to them.

The main road through Berry is Highway 18, which ends twenty miles to the west in Fayette, the county seat. Until a few years ago the first thing you would notice when driving through Berry was the wedge-shaped Cannon Store, sitting in the point where the railroad track intersects the highway at an angle. To fit as large a mercantile store as he could on his triangular lot, Mr. Cannon built a three-story, three-sided building. He covered it in silvery sheet metal and painted big, neat letters on the front saying "Theron Cannon & Company— We Handle Most Everything from a Cradle to a Coffin." Cannon's is gone now but in its time it held cotton seed, fertilizer, roofing material, nails, bolts of cloth, straw hats, shoes, mules, wagons, radios, buttons, candy, and yes—cradles and coffins. Next to it, in the larger part of the triangle made by the railroad tracks, was Shepherd's, a mercantile store with four sides. Sharecroppers had accounts at one or the other of these stores and folks say you could tell which store a farmer patronized by the brand of overalls he wore. Shepherd's is gone, too, but when we moved to Berry those two stores stocked every item that we knew to exist in the world.

Beyond those two buildings and across the tracks was downtown Berry. There was the Yellow Front store, which sold clothes; the Bank of Berry, a grocery store, a drug store, a shoe shop, one or two little cafes, a doctor's office, a dentist's office, a barbershop, a beauty shop, and the post office. There used to be a movie theater in Berry where the bank is now, but one night while they were showing a film, it caught on fire. The whole thing burned down and took a couple of other stores with it. Berry had its own taxi company and the Miss-Ala bus line stopped there. On the other side of Highway18, across from Cannon's and Shepherd's, were a couple of churches, the elementary school, and some of the nicer houses, though there certainly weren't any mansions in Berry. Surrounding the town were the places where most men in Berry worked—a couple of big saw mills, some box factories, and a few small coal mines, the kind where all the digging was done by hand. I suppose Berry was a town by definition—it had about 1,500 people—but most of the folks who lived there had big gardens in their yards and kept chickens and cows.

In Berry I could walk to the same school I had taken the school bus to when we lived in the country. I passed right through downtown to get there. One time when I had done something for Daddy, he gave me some money, maybe a dime. I had never heard of bubble gum before we came to Berry but the children there loved it. I stopped at Shepherd's that morning and bought a pocketful of Dubble Bubble. I was the most popular girl in the second grade that day—for a couple of hours, anyway.

The country children rode the bus to school and once they were there they couldn't leave the school grounds to go to town unless their parents sent a permission slip. They may have needed coffee, for instance, and they'd just give the child some money that morning and say "Go on your lunch break and get a pound of coffee." But no child had permission to leave the school to buy bubble gum and everyone really wanted that gum when they saw mine. So I sold it to them. When the teacher discovered that those children were short on their lunch money she made me give their pennies back, even though they had already chewed up and spit out my gum.

That February my youngest sister Doris was born at home with the help of the town doctor, my grandmother Whitson, and one of mother's sisters. The rest of us stayed with a neighbor until Daddy came to get us and told us we had a baby sister. She turned out to be a pretty child—bright and into everything. So now our family consisted of Mother, Daddy, five children and our faithful dog Butch.

By and large our life in Berry was safe and pleasant and much easier than it had been in the country. For one thing, we didn't have to haul water from the creek. There was a well between our house and the one next door. Having a good clean well, under a big apple tree close to our kitchen, was a real luxury. Before long, however, it became a source of deep pain for Daddy and his children.

We shared our well and cow pasture with Widow Hyde and her son John. Mrs. Hyde and her late husband had been well respected and seemed to have more money, or at least a nicer house, than the rest of us. John Hyde had been married and had served for a little while in World War II. The war was still on, but he was back in Berry, divorced and living with his mother. If John ever worked I never did know it. He was home all the time and I guess he got fascinated with that attractive woman whose cow pastured with his.

Suddenly my mother started disappearing for long hours during the day. Daddy didn't notice at first because he wasn't home a lot himself. If the mill needed a load of lumber delivered to Tuscaloosa, or Jasper, or Columbus, Mississippi, or Birmingham, Daddy would deliver it and might not come home at noon for dinner or for supper that evening. But occasionally if he was at the mill, he'd drop by during the day and more than once all he found was Doris, who wasn't a year old yet, crawling around on the floor attended only by me, eight years old; my six-year-old sister, and two little brothers.

Mother wasn't there and we didn't know where she was. When she showed up she would have excuses about what she had been doing but they seldom panned out. So Daddy told me to watch what was going on.

It didn't take me long to figure out that the well had something to do with Mother's disappearances. Usually she sent me to draw water, but there were times that she went herself and I noticed that when that happened John also came to the well. He was lazy, so for him to haul water was something out of the ordinary. There was a big flat rock beside the well that we sat our buckets on to keep the bottoms clean. From the kitchen window I would see Mother putting a note in a hollowed out place under that rock and just a little while later John would arrive, raise the rock and take the note out. I suppose she was telling him a meeting place, for she would be gone the rest of the day.

At first Daddy didn't believe me when I told him what was happening. But one day he arrived right after Mother had left. I told him that I had just seen her write something on a sheet of paper, fold it up, and take it to the well. He didn't say anything but he got his .22 rifle and waited at the kitchen window. When John showed up and stooped to pick up the note, Daddy shot it out of his hand. He just stood in the window and fired, but he was too good a shot to hit what he didn't intend to. John high-tailed it out of there and Daddy retrieved the note.

A year of heated battles between Mother and Daddy followed. They didn't divorce right away because Daddy wanted to work things out and make her love him again. Mother said that she wanted to get a job. There was no need for her to go to work—Daddy made good money according to what people lived on back then—but she just didn't want parental responsibilities. So he let her go off to work at the Berry Box Company where she helped assemble wooden crates that were used to ship ammunition and other war materials in. He even bought her a late 1930s coupe to drive herself to work in. I think she was the only woman in Berry who knew how to drive. Daddy would take Esta and Milford to stay at his Mama and Papa's house in the country, and I would be in charge of Karrold and Doris while Mother was at work. But there were times that all of them were my responsibility.

Mother didn't prepare meals ahead for us or even make sure there was anything in the house for us to eat while she was at work. I can remember feeding us raw oatmeal—just pouring oat meal out in a bowl and putting milk on it because I didn't know any better. And cooking was hard for me because all we had was a wood stove. I could not reach the pans on top of it without burning my arm. Daddy built me a step to stand on when I cooked. That was the way Daddy was; he could solve technical problems like helping me reach the stovetop but he wasn't disturbed by the fact that a small child had to do all the cooking for the rest of his children. So there I was building fires and cooking for four younger ones with no one but Butch to look after us.

And things happened that summer that I guess I'll take with me to the grave. How we kept from drowning or getting eaten up by snakes, I'll never know. But nobody cared.

I remember one particular day when it was so hot that all we could think of was swimming, though none of us could really swim. After lunch, disregarding everything we had been told, we headed down to the branch at the back side of our pasture. It was shallow but had little pools we could sit down in. We put Doris on a quilt, ran down the bank, and splashed into the water. After some minutes of noisy horseplay Karrold turned around and said, "Where's Doris?" She wasn't where we'd left her. And about that time, her head bobbed up in one of the pools. She wasn't making a sound, a sure sign that she was drowning. We got her out before any damage was done, but it scared us enough that we didn't try that again.

Another time we had one of those notorious West Alabama thunderstorms that turn the sky solid black. It was midnight-dark in the house and we didn't want to be there by ourselves. We wanted Mother. As the lightning grew sharper we panicked and headed out to find her. I took Milford on my back and Esta put Doris on hers. I grabbed Karrold's hand and we started running toward Box Factory Road through a ferocious storm. There was no one to tell us any different.

It was raining bucketsful as we passed Mrs. Meadows' little row house. Mrs. Meadow's husband was paralyzed from a stroke and mumbled to the point where you couldn't understand anything he said. Their only child, people said, was retarded. I didn't understand disabilities like that and I avoided the whole family. But when Mrs. Meadows saw us coming up the street in the middle of a thunderstorm, she came out and made us stay in her house until it had passed. Even though I was afraid of her, I was more afraid of the thunder and lightning.

Then there was the time Mother left me to do the laundry by myself. This involved getting water from the well, putting it in the wash pot, building a fire under it, boiling the clothes, scrubbing them on a rub board, rinsing them in fresh water, wringing them out by hand, and on and on. I did it all but I couldn't reach the clothesline to hang them out to dry. When Mother saw that I had hung them on a rusty barbed wire pasture fence, she whipped me until the blood ran down my legs.

Another time—I don't remember if this is before she went to work or afterwards—we washed the clothes together. After we finished, Mother told me to bring a bucket of the boiling water from the wash pot into the house to scrub the floor with. Everyone washed their wooden floors with the laundry water because the lye soap in it would bleach them out. As I was bringing it in, I tripped and filled both of my shoes with boiling hot water. Wouldn't a real mother scoop me up, hug me, and check my feet to see if they were burned? Mine cursed me for being careless and whipped me.

I never did understand Mother as long as she lived. She had more possessions than any other women we knew at the time, but she just didn't have any self-satisfaction. She had two personalities. At one moment she could be a hard-working woman going about household business very efficiently and at the next she would let you know she hated you with a vengeance. I never knew which one she would be at any given moment.

When she did something nice there was usually a hidden motive, such as the time she took us in her car to a public swimming area in a creek outside of Berry. It wasn't long before John Hyde arrived and sat on a quilt beside my mother while we splashed in the water.

Such incidents made Daddy realize that the arrangements in Berry were not working, for suddenly he moved us five or six miles out of town into a lonely old house, with unpainted, weathered board siding. It sat on a rise and had a high-pitched roof that gave it a haunted look. There were no neighbors in sight and there was no well—to get water we had to walk to a branch a long ways through the woods. There were no electric lights, so we started going to bed when it got dark. None of us wanted to mess with coal oil lamps.

Daddy had made mother quit her job and she was supposed to be staying home with us, but she started sneaking off again and more battles followed. The last night they were together Mother cooked a nice supper for Daddy. I can't remember anything she fixed except the biscuits and gravy. I was sitting near Mother at one end of the table and Karrold sat near Daddy at the other. She sat a large plate of biscuits at our end and gave Daddy his own small plate. Karrold reached over to Daddy's plate for a biscuit and when he did, Mother slapped it out of his hand, saying "Those aren't your biscuits! Put that one back." Daddy smelled a rat.

"Did you put poison in these biscuits?"

She didn't answer. Daddy took a pistol out of one of the pockets of his overalls and asked her again. I don't know what she replied because I rushed my brothers and sisters into another room where we couldn't see or hear what was going on. All I know is that Mother left that night and never came back, and I mean *never*.

So suddenly Daddy, a young man, maybe 30 years old, had sole responsibility for five children and no idea how to take care of us. He talked one of Mother's nieces into staying with us for a few days until he could make other arrangements. Her husband worked with Daddy at the sawmill. For a short while she and her husband and two boys were with us in the old country house. The men would get up and go off to work in the morning and she would stay with us through the day. But I could tell she didn't want to be there. One afternoon when one of her boys got sick, her husband came and took all of them home, leaving me and my little brood alone in a creepy house.

We didn't know what to do with ourselves at first, but we were out of water and needed to haul some to the house before dark. I wasn't sure how to get to the branch but I knew that whatever we did, we needed to stay together. I picked up two water buckets and handed one to Karrold. I told Esta to tote Doris and to hold Milford's hand while we went to the spring. Even with Butch along I was nervous the whole time. When we returned with our water I remember building a fire in the stove and fixing us something for supper though I can't imagine what it was. After it got dark and Daddy had not come home, we really began to feel uneasy. All of us, at one point or another, cried because we were by ourselves.

The only thing to do was go to sleep but none of us wanted to sleep in our own beds. The one bed large enough to hold us all was very high off the floor and I remember trying to decide how we were all going to sleep on it without Doris falling off. Somehow we managed to pull the mattress off the bed and onto the floor. Before we got on it we pushed chairs against the doors to keep anyone from coming in on us, since the house had no locks. Then we all huddled together crossways on the bed—and Butch stayed beside us.

When Daddy finally came home in the wee hours of the morning, Butch tried to tear him up. Of course, Daddy didn't know we were by ourselves. I feel like if he had known what was happening he would have come home directly instead of hauling lumber to Birmingham or Tuscaloosa or wherever he'd been. The next day he went to talk to his father and mother and that evening he carried us out to their farm.

It was late when we got to my grandparents' house. They had a good-sized fire in the fireplace but the rest of the house was dark, since my grandmother would not burn electric lights or kerosene lanterns at night. They were sitting beside the fire and when we came in, grandmother, in her orderly fashion, set everyone down and proceeded to give us a lecture, punctuated with the sizzle of spurts of snuff hitting the flames.

"You are going to live here now," she said, "and it's going to be hard on Papa and me because you are all heathens. You never learned any manners and don't even know how to say 'Yes Ma'am,' 'No, Ma'am' or 'Yes, Sir', 'No, Sir.' You haven't learned the first commandment, have you? Do you know what that is? In my house the first commandment is to do whatever I say and don't question it. But it is going to be different now and you will learn it." Then she said something that Milford and I still talk about: "If you are going to live in this house, you are going to do what I say and if I tell you to jump, you jump even if it's into this fireplace." All we could think about was roasting in that huge fireplace. I was sure she was not exaggerating for effect. She never said anything she didn't mean. ❧

This photo of Julia and Jesse Whitson (Mama and Papa) was taken after all of their grandchildren had left, probably around 1960. Mama still kept her floors immaculate and Papa still raised his feist dogs.

Basic Training

So in the Fall of 1945 we began living with our grandparents on a farm 15 miles out of Berry. My grandmother, Julia Whitson, was 53 years old at the time but seemed much older than that with her stern, old-fashioned ways and her gray hair pulled back into a bun. Her husband, Jesse Whitson, was a few years older than she, but seemed younger. Together they had raised six children—Aaron, Edward, Theron, Bradley, Ezzie, and Lois—all married now and living elsewhere in Fayette County, except for Daddy who had suddenly returned home with five more children and a dog for them to raise. I must have had some hope for a loving relationship with them when we first moved there, for I asked if we could call them Mama and Papa, like our Daddy did, instead of Grandmother and Grandfather. We were allowed to do so, but we never felt the kind of affection that you'd expect with words like Mama and Papa.

Papa had always been a tenant farmer and moved his family from one man's farm to another until Aunt Bell Fowler's family gave him the opportunity to be a landowner. Bell Fowler was a widow who lived by herself on a farm. She had been an active, independent woman, but now she was old, cantankerous, and needed someone to take care of her. No one in her family wanted to take her on. One of the Fowlers made it known that if he could find the right person to care for her the rest of her life, that person would inherit her house and property. My grandparents were still farming at the Sexton's—where Mother and Daddy met—when they heard about the offer. Mama moved there right away and the rest of the family joined her after they got the crops in. Aunt Bell was ornery, but she met her match in my grandmother. The Fowlers kept their word and deeded the house and 120-acre farm over to Mama and Papa when Aunt Bell passed.

It was a simple, unpainted farmhouse, but in later years, after the children were grown and before we invaded it, Papa and his sons built on a new kitchen with hand-made cabinets and plenty of windows and bought an electric stove and refrigerator. Mama was very proud of that kitchen and kept it spotless. In my grandparents' house we had good food to eat and clean clothes to wear, but I have to say that my years there were not happy ones. Mama was one of the sternest disciplinarians that God ever let live and I was afraid of her. There was no leeway in her sense of right and wrong and she didn't have an ounce of fun in her. She never hugged anybody, never told anybody she loved them, never showed any affection. And having been abandoned by our mother, we longed for all those things. On the other hand, I cherish all I learned from my grandparents. Their farm was a model of self-sufficiency. They did every chore with care and skill and they made sure that we did the same. There's not a day that goes by that I don't use something they taught me.

When we moved to the farm in 1945, people in Berry and Fayette could buy refrigerators, hot water heaters, wringer washers, electric ranges with push button controls and automatic timer ovens, every known brand of American car and truck, and Coca Colas bottled right there in Fayette. Not Mama and Papa—they had electricity but used it sparingly, not allowing themselves to exceed the $1 per month flat rate on the power bill. They still farmed with mules and when they went anywhere, those mules pulled them in a wagon. But since they grew or made most of what they needed themselves, they rarely went anywhere. What they didn't grow, like sugar, salt, black pepper, coffee, and snuff, Mama got at the rolling store that came to us from Berry every Tuesday.

At Mama and Papa's we went to the same school we had walked to in Berry, but now we rode the bus that picked us up two miles from the house. Everything that we did during the school week revolved around that long walk to and from the bus stop. We had to get up early enough to get all our chores done and still catch the bus on time. Papa arose long before dawn. In cold weather the first thing he did was stoke the fire in the fireplace. Then he'd go into the kitchen and start up Mama's Home Comfort wood stove where all the meals were cooked, since she preferred it to the electric range. Next he would wake up my grandmother, Esta, and me but leave the little ones sleeping while we did the chores. Papa and I would grab a kerosene lantern because it was still dark, take the bucket that was hanging on the back porch filled with leftovers from the night before, and throw the slops and some grain to the hogs. After we fed the cows and mules, I milked our cow Peggy and Papa milked his while Mama and Esta were cooking up a big breakfast. After eating we cleaned up the kitchen, made our beds, got dressed and set off for the school bus. This schedule was as automatic as breathing; there was no deviation.

We got out of school at three in the afternoon and the trip home took about an hour. By the time we walked home from the bus it was almost dark, but we still had chores to do. Our drinking and cooking water came from a spring about a half a mile from the house. We had a well on the porch, but we used it only for washing dishes and baths because Mama did not think it was sanitary. It took all of us children two or three trips to the spring, with everybody carrying two buckets apiece to get the water needed for the next 24 hours. And we had to put in firewood and stove wood each night to last through the next day. Getting enough wood to cook two meals on a wood stove plus keep a fire going all day in the fireplace was a major job. The fireplace was enormous and Papa burned logs that were at least four feet long. We divided up the chores and while some of us were hauling wood and water, the rest were feeding the animals and milking the cows for the second time that day.

Mama had some chores she did by herself. She fed the chickens and tended to the hens when they were hatching and raising their chicks. And in the afternoon she gathered eggs. She didn't trust us with those; they were money in her pocket at the rolling store. But the other chores were ours to do whether it interfered with homework or not. Education was not a top priority with Mama and Papa. You were expected to bring in decent grades and were in trouble if you didn't, but no one reminded you to do your homework or set aside time for you to do it. I remember a night that I needed to study for a test but hadn't found time that afternoon. Mama did not let us burn the lights at night so after we ate supper, I sat by the fireplace and studied until Papa banked the fire. I went to bed worried and after everybody else had gone to sleep, I got up. It was a bright, clear night, so I gathered up my books, slipped outside and sat on the end of the porch by the well. I've forgotten how I did on the test, but I still remember how elated I felt as I studied by moonlight even though I was terrified that Mama would discover me doing something so out of the ordinary and, in her mind, needless.

Walking to and from the bus had its pluses and minuses. Doris and Milford were still too young to go to school, but Karrold, Esta, and I would set off on foot each morning even if it were pouring down rain. There was no car sitting in the driveway to take us to the bus stop and we didn't have raincoats, boots, or umbrellas, so if we got wet we just wore our wet clothes in class until they dried. On nice days, though, walking to the bus was playtime. At Mama's house we weren't allowed to have childish ways. She didn't put up with it. On the way to the bus, though, we could run, laugh, throw rocks and do whatever we wanted to because no one else was around. Butch would horse around with us and we would send him back when we reached the road. We'd take our slingshots and hide them before we got to the bus stop—they weren't allowed at school—and on the way home we'd uncover them and shoot anything that moved. Papa could kill a grasshopper in flight with a slingshot and we tried to be like him.

Most of the time we carried our lunches to school, since Mama and Papa didn't have cash to pay for us to eat in the lunchroom, and I don't think Daddy was contributing much for our upkeep. My sack lunch was usually a biscuit with whatever we had left over from breakfast or maybe peanut butter and crackers. Most of the time we had something sweet in there because on Saturdays we would make enough teacakes or gingerbread or fried pies to last through the week. Ours were made with homemade sorghum syrup instead of sugar. Mama knew just exactly how much to bake to last us a week. A cake would last so many days, cookies would last so many days. I especially liked the teacakes. She made a fudgy chocolate filling and we'd stick two cookies together with it, our homemade version of Oreos. A lot of what I know about cooking comes from baking with Mama on Saturdays.

When we knew the lunchroom was going to have some special meal, like turkey and dressing before Thanksgiving, we'd carry fresh vegetables or jars of canned food to school to pay for our lunch. The lunchroom workers lived in the area and knew who grew what and what the sanitary conditions were like on each farm. They had specific people they would ask to bring food to school. Papa was famous for his sweet potatoes, so they would have us bring some from time to time. We would lug a bushel basket, one of us on each side, up to the bus and haul it into the school. Sometimes we would pick baskets of turnip greens in the afternoon and carry them to school the next morning; at other times it might be milk and eggs or butter. In return we would get some free lunches and take home a little cash for Papa.

I remember one time when my class was planning a field trip. We were going to walk to a pond not very far from the school and we were all supposed to bring sack lunches. Mama decided to bake some bread so that I could have a sandwich instead of a biscuit that day. Most of the other mothers had gone to the store and bought white bread for the occasion, and when we sat down to eat, one of my classmates laughed and pointed out to the class that I had home-made bread. He knew because it wasn't as pale white and thinly sliced as everybody else's. My teacher, Mrs. McCracken, saw how embarrassed I was and told the class that I was the only one with someone who loved them enough to make homemade bread for their lunch. It was a nice try but it didn't lessen the pain a bit. First of all, I would have loved to have store-bought bread like everyone else and second, I knew for sure that Mama didn't love me.

Of course, we had all been dumped on her. She had finished

raising her family and just when she should have been able to relax a bit, she suddenly had five more bodies to feed, bathe, and provide beds and clean clothes for, with little help from our father. At that time Daddy was working on the road crew that was building Highway 102 and he was gone most of the time. I guess I shouldn't have expected Mama to be all smiles and hugs, but at the same time, it was not our fault that we were there. A little compassion would have helped, but none came. 🐦

Mama

To go from living on our own, mostly unsupervised, to living with Mama required an adjustment of the worst kind. I doubt military school could have been any harsher. I'm grateful for everything that I learned from her, which really shaped my life, but the lessons would have been better if gently taught. Instead everything was cold and businesslike. She read the Bible and her favorite book in it was Leviticus with all its strict laws about diet, dress, and conduct. Above all, she believed that cleanliness was next to Godliness. If that is true, Julia Whitson is most assuredly sitting at the right hand of God today.

I've heard so many people say "You could eat off of Julie's kitchen floor." She swept her floors every day—not just the floors, but under beds and anything that could be moved. In the summer and on weekends, sweeping was our job. The floor planks ran long ways of the house and we had to sweep with the grain, so we could get any trash out of the cracks. Sometimes I swept the same room as many as four or five times before I got it the way she wanted. If she saw dirt between the cracks we kept after it until it was gone.

Each of our beds had a feather mattress and a cotton mattress that were rotated according to the season. If it was wintertime the feather mattress was on top and the cotton mattress underneath and vice versa in the summertime. They laid on top of a frame of open coils that sat on slats. When it was time to rotate the mattresses she went after every speck of dust that might be on those coils. And every day she made her bed up straight and tight, like a military cot. We didn't dare touch her bed because our fingers might make dents in the covers and we'd get a whipping. She expected ours to look like hers and if they didn't, she would strip everything off and make us do it again and again until we got it right.

We churned every day because we had two cows. Even with seven or eight of us eating there each day and Daddy's two sisters in town coming to get milk and butter on the weekend, there was still enough milk to make the butter that Mama sold to the rolling store. Churning is a messy job, but Mama didn't allow messes and we learned the hard way not to lift the dasher all the way up and plunge it down with a splash. She was fastidious with her milk. Most people strained milk through screen wire or milk strainers, but we strained ours through flour sacks that had been washed and bleached and kept apart from the rest of the laundry. She'd take the butter out of the churn with the dasher or a spoon. Her daughter Ezzie remembers Mama telling about visiting some of her relatives and seeing one of them take up butter with her hands. When it came time for Mama to go home, Aunt So-and-So gave her a biscuit with that fresh butter. Mama held it in her hand until she got outside the house then threw it away.

She was meticulous about everything she did. Once a year she made her own soap and she knew just how much to make to last through a year of baths, dishwashing and laundry. There was no Ivory Liquid, no Clorox bleach, no White Rain shampoo in the Whitson house, just two kinds of lye soap—hard and soft. When it came time to make the lye, Mama would let the fire die down completely in the fireplace, then sweep it until it looked like you could have a picnic in it. She would build a hickory or oak fire and keep it burning until she had enough ashes to fill a hopper. During that time we could not burn anything Mama considered unclean. Mama and Papa couldn't even spit their snuff into the fireplace like they usually did. When she got the ash hopper full, she started a process of pouring water through it. Homemade lye, a stinging reddish-brown liquid, would trickle out the other end. To make her soap, she would take a wash pot, add a portion of the fat she'd rendered when the hogs were slaughtered, add lye, and cook it to a certain stage. The soap that was going to be used for washing hands and the like, she would pour into a pan, let it harden and cut it into bars. The other she put in jugs and used for laundry.

The laundry, of course, had its rules. The day before you washed clothes, you drew water from the clearest part of the spring and let it sit overnight so that the dregs could settle before you poured it into the wash pot.

When I describe Mama now it seems like she was a model of skill, efficiency and economy, but if you had been near her at the time you would have called her a fanatic. Aunt Ezzie said that Mama became more extreme after her own children grew up and they built the new kitchen onto the back of the house. Mama's kitchen was her sacred space with its polished pine floors, bright windows, and beloved Home Comfort stove. She kept that stove polished to a high luster all the time. A wet rag never touched it—only a clean, dry cloth would suffice. She didn't allow anything to boil over on it and we couldn't stir while we were cooking because we might spill a drop of grease on it. Instead we had to move the pot to the table, stir it, and then put it back on the stove.

Aunt Ezzie said that when she would go home to visit, she'd go into the kitchen to help and Mama would watch her like a hawk, because she knew Ezzie was a natural born haphazard and liable to make a mess. She finally quit going in the kitchen because she realized she was making Mama nervous.

Mama was the same about the front yard. A lot of the people around us had dirt yards they swept with brush brooms. We did that in back but we also had a big front yard with grass outlined by flowerbeds and fences. It was our job to groom it immaculately using a rotary-type push mower and a swing blade. Cutting the grass was a two-day chore for us kids, done once a week during the summer. Yard work was the way she kept us busy and the way she punished us. In the summertime, if we got all our chores done, she would send us out along the edge of the fields to cut weeds. Or if we displeased her in some way we had to spend extra hours cutting ragweed away from the outhouse and the path that went to it. That was mild punishment.

For worse crimes, there was the hickory in the kitchen or whatever was nearby, be it a stick of firewood or a chair. When

Mama started whipping, she didn't know when to stop. Sometimes she would fly off the handle and whip the whole bunch of us when she had finished with the main culprit. I remember one day when she was canning beans and I did something to warrant a whipping. She called me in and said, "I'm going to give you a whipping when I get time. I don't have time now to give it to you." Well, I was the best little thing you've ever seen the rest of the day. I worked all day long, did everything she said, went through the routines of supper and getting everybody washed and ready for bed. There was no bathtub—the only time we bathed was when we went to the branch, and we only did that in the summer time—but in Mama's house you had to get a really good rag bath every night. She would not let you get in one of her beds if you weren't clean. So part of my routine was getting Doris and Milford cleaned up and into their beds. That night when I had them tucked away I said to myself, "I've got it made. She forgot to whip me." I was sound asleep when she came in, stood beside the bed, turned the cover back, and said, "I'm going to give you your whipping." It was not the token whipping you'd expect after her anger had cooled; it was a hard, mean whipping. When she finished she said, " Now go back to bed and go to sleep."

Of course, these whippings caused problems with Butch, who was, as Milford said, "bad particular." When we lived in Berry, he wouldn't let anyone come in the yard if we kids were outside. If a stranger tried to take a shortcut through our property, he'd leave without part of his trousers. One day when grandmother was whipping Karrold with a switch, Butch got hold of the hand she had the switch in. He wasn't trying to attack her; he just wanted her to quit. She took us all inside and Butch burst through the screen door after us. So he was always on Mama's bad side. 🦋

Papa

Papa was a small, nice-looking man with a youthful face. Most of the time he was easy-going and loved to play pranks on people. He would take you fishing or tell you a joke, things that Mama would never do. He had a little feist named Boots who went everywhere with him. Feists are small, wiry dogs that country folks favor. They are similar to rat terriers or Jack Russell terriers, but they aren't purebred dogs. If a dog is little, fast, and goes after squirrels, people will call it a feist. Boots stayed in the barn at night but during the day he went to the fields and hunted for rats and snakes or slept in the shade while Papa worked.

Papa liked to play tricks on us. One time when we hadn't been there very long he sent Karrold and me to get something out of the mule barn. He didn't tell us that the mules would chase us but if we turned around and said boo to them, they'd go the other way. Suddenly we saw two galloping mules coming at us at breakneck speed. We flew over the fence without touching any boards and there stood Papa laughing at us.

I remember late one summer when Papa, Karrold and I were across the road laying by cotton. That means we were plowing it for the last time before leaving it to mature until harvest. Karrold and I were cutting the tall weeds out and Papa was running between the rows with his Georgia stock and sweep, throwing dirt up on the base of the plants. When Karrold and I finished and were heading home, we saw a huge snake slither out of the cotton patch and into the yard. With hoes in hand, we chased him across the yard into some rose bushes. We poked at him through the bushes with our hoes until he decided he'd had enough and started to come out after us. We yelled so much that Papa stopped the mule and came across the road to see what all the commotion was about. He tapped the snake on the head with one of the hoes and killed it. Then he pulled it out and stretched it out across the yard; it had to be every bit of five feet long. He said it was a coachwhip and wasn't poisonous.

"Now come here, I'm going to show you how to tell what it is." We bent down close to the snake, intent on Papa's lesson, but then I noticed the tip of the hoe going up under that snake and I knew one of us was fixing to wear it. I took off running toward the house and Karrold went up the hill. I had on a dress because my Old-Testament grandmother did not allow her girls to wear men's clothing, and I was running and hollering just as loud as I could holler. About the time I got even with the porch I felt that snake hit the side of my neck and slide inside the front of my dress. I was running full force and it got tangled in my legs as it dropped out the bottom of the dress and onto the ground. Papa was dying laughing and I was screaming bloody murder. Well, about that time Mama came out of the house. She thought one of us was dead, I guess. When she saw what had happened, she stood on the porch and preached a sermon to Papa that would burn the Devil's ears. He went back and plowed and didn't come home for dinner that night. I guess he didn't figure it was safe.

Papa was gifted with a slingshot. In the summertime grasshoppers would sit out on gravel roads. When you got near them they would rise a few feet off the ground. Papa could put a round rock about the size of a dime in his slingshot, draw back, and knock that grasshopper out of mid air. Mama's pride and joy were her chickens, and she had roosters that Papa absolutely hated. Sometimes when we were feeding the chickens in the evening he liked to infuriate Mama by using his slingshot to keep those roosters away from the feed.

We had a little branch that ran through the bottom that we called Clear Creek. In the summertime a thundershower could come up and within twenty minutes that creek would just be rolling muddy. If you waited an hour, it would clear up again. About the only kind of fish it had in it were mud cats and bream. They are little fish with red stripes on them and are really good eating. If it rained, Papa would take us fishing. We'd go to the barn, get our cane poles—we'd never heard of a rod and reel—and fill a Prince Albert tobacco tin full of red worms. Then we'd try to catch us a mess of fish.

Papa didn't punish us as often as Mama did, but when he did you knew you'd been to the woodshed. Like Mama he didn't repeat what he told you to do. He expected it to be done on the first go-round. As far as I remember, the only time that he ever whipped me was for not getting out of bed right away. Every morning he would get the fires going, then tell us to get up. There was a hickory switch over the kitchen sink and if you didn't get up after he had called you a couple of times, he'd go get it. You know how warm and comfortable you are in bed that time of morning and the house around you is so cold that you just want to snuggle down in the covers and stay there? Once I went sound asleep after he'd called me and he pulled off the covers and popped me with that switch. Except for that one time I always heard him when he scooted his chair up and started toward the kitchen sink. Before he'd get back with that switch, I'd be out of bed.

He was harder on the boys than on me. Milford remembers one time when he was about five years old and was toting water from the branch to the house in two three-quart Golden Eagle syrup buckets. He accidentally knocked a small hole in one of them and when he got to the house he didn't have but a half jug of water. Papa saw that hole in the jug, went out and cut a good-sized limb and flew into whipping. He whipped and whipped until blood was running down Milford's legs and splattering on the porch. Finally Mama came out of the kitchen carrying an old shotgun. She stuck that barrel right in Papa's ear and said, "Jesse Whitson, you hit that boy again and I'll kill you." He threw the limb out in the yard and turned around and walked off. Milford laid on his belly for two or three days. But when Mama got mad, she would do the same thing. ❧

Food

Life at Mama and Papa's was a mixture of harshness and beauty. Though Mama's severity made me miserable much of the time, I was fascinated by my grandparents' deep knowledge of how to grow, gather, and preserve all the food that we ate. Even at nine or ten years old I was proud of their skill and wanted to learn all they knew.

Papa always raised hogs and killed two or three each fall to keep us in meat for a year. Mama rendered the lard and used it for cooking and soap making. She also ground her own sausage meat, mixed in salt, homegrown sage and dried red pepper, and stuffed it into tube bags that she had cut and stitched from flour sacks. Papa smoked the sausage along with bacon and ham that had been cured in salt. The smokehouse was just off the kitchen and every morning Mama would get whatever meat she wanted out of it for our big breakfast. With it we'd have eggs, biscuits and gravy, or biscuits with butter, jelly, or sorghum syrup. We kept homemade sorghum syrup in pottery jugs with clean white rags as stoppers and used it in all the sweets we baked.

Our breakfasts were hardy but the noon meal, dinner, was the main meal of the day. Mainly we ate boiled or fried vegetables with cornbread and milk or water. And for supper, we'd just eat leftovers from dinner. We'd have whatever was in season. In the spring there would be English peas, carrots, early turnip greens, and Irish potatoes. We loved fried potatoes. They had a special taste because they were cooked in lard in heavy iron skillets—no vegetable oil and Teflon for us. In the summer we had green beans, tomatoes, corn, butter beans, and several kinds of field peas. In the fall and part of the winter we ate mustard greens, a second batch of turnip greens and turnips, collards and sweet potatoes. Papa grew tons of sweet potatoes. When we dug them in the fall, we'd pile them up in a little shed, then cover them with pine straw and shovel dirt on top to keep them from freezing. We ate them until everything else started coming in the next spring. Mama cut them into chunks and steamed them with butter and sorghum and served them for dinner, or she would bake a big pan full of them, all the oven could hold, and we would eat them for a couple of days. And she would make sweet potato pies or use them as a filling for fried pies.

We didn't grow the kind of sweet corn that most people prefer today. It doesn't can well, so we didn't have a way to keep it. But we grew and ate plenty of starchy field corn, cooked cream-style. We planted enough corn to feed ourselves, the cows, mules, and chickens, and we ground the rest into corn meal. And every year Mama would make a wash pot full of hominy, using dried corn and her homemade lye. Of course, we didn't throw the cobs away. They became stove wood.

In the winter we ate up the vegetables we had spent the summer canning. Mama and Papa always made a big vegetable garden outside the house where they planted all the things that had to be protected from rabbits and other creatures. It had a fence around it that they grew butter beans on. Mama planned the garden so that not everything came in at one time. There were just so many hands to wash, snap, string, or slice the vegetables. She would calculate that the green beans would be in this week and we'd have two weeks to can them before the peas would be ready, and the corn would come in after that. We picked only the amount of beans that we could can that day along with all the other chores we had to do. Mama could figure the amount she needed down to a half a cup. It amazed me at how well she could go out there and pick just enough vegetables. "Now this is going to be two cookers full and I don't need any more."

When we had time, we would put up shelly beans. Those were beans that were almost dried and had turned yellow. They were tough and couldn't be snapped, so they had to be shelled, which was pretty labor intensive. When we picked them there were usually some green beans still on the vine. We'd mix them, half shelly beans and half green snap beans. Those were so good that we usually saved them for company.

Mama grew strawberries that she turned into jam and we picked bucketsful of blackberries that she preserved for cobblers. We also dried immense amounts of fruit. We'd peel and slice apples and lay them out on two or three pieces of tin to dry. And we had little Indian peaches by the tubful. They were clear-stone peaches, not much bigger than a hickory nut. We would wash them, cut a little ring round the top of each one, pop the pit out, and lay them out to dry. Mama took those fruits and the beans that we had let dry on the vine, put them in sacks, and hung them on the edge of the porch outside. She dropped some snuff in them to keep the insects out and left them there until after the meats were smoked and she could move them to the smokehouse.

There were three kinds of beans Mama liked to dry—white, black, and striped cornfield beans. They had more bean and less hull than other varieties. Since she saved some of this year's beans to make next year's crop, she was meticulous in planting them. She would put one variety in the vegetable garden and the others in fields some distance from each other so they wouldn't get cross-pollinated by the bees and turn into some other variety.

About the only frivolous things we grew were peanuts and popcorn. We'd make popcorn balls and peanut brittle with Papa's sorghum syrup, so we didn't have to go out and buy anything for a treat. Also we had walnut trees and gathered baskets of black walnuts in the fall. Before Christmas we would sit around the fireplace and pick the meat out for Mama to use in cookies and cakes.

Needless to say, we didn't come by all this food without effort. During the summer we got in the field soon after daylight and worked there until the sun was directly overhead, our signal that it was time to go home for dinner. We ate and rested for about an hour. That break was more for the mules than us. Then we'd go back to the field and work until the sun went down. While we were at Mama and Papa's the institution of daylight savings time came into being. Never was a clock on the farm changed. We stayed on the same schedule regardless of what the rest of the world did. We got up by the crack of dawn and went to bed when it got dark and what everyone else did was up to them. ❧

Fieldwork

When we moved to Mama and Papa's I was the only child big enough to hold a plow stock. This was one instance where being the oldest was an advantage; it meant that I could work in the fields with Papa instead of in the house with Mama. I got a real education in caring for our land, making it richer, and getting the most out of every inch of it that we could, besides having fun with Papa.

I wasn't tall enough to hold the plow by the handles but I could grab the crossbar and do everything that Papa did. Because he was short, he worked small mules that some call mining mules. I plowed with Ada and Papa worked with Joe. Ada was gentle and so methodical that she would just follow Joe and do whatever he did. I didn't have to give any commands.

Each year before we planted any crops we would fertilize the fields. Papa would order a truckload of 8-8-8 chemical fertilizer on credit from the feed store and pay for it in the fall when he sold the cotton. We called it "gu-anner" and I never knew why it had that strange name. Someone told me a few years back that it's really called guano (pronounced "gwano") and it means bat dung, which people used to dig out of caves to fertilize their crops. Papa bought gu-anner for the fields, but in our vegetable garden we used manure from the barn. We'd put it on after the garden was finished in the fall and let it compost over the winter before we planted again.

We did a lot of double crops. For instance, when the field corn that we planted for animal feed would get knee or thigh high, it was time to lay it by. That's the time we'd plant peas or cornfield beans between the stalks. Papa would give me a bucketful of ammonia— we called it soda—and I would put a tablespoonful of it at the base of each cornstalk. Then Papa would come through with his turning plow and throw up a little bed of dirt that I'd strow with seeds we'd saved out from last year's crop. When he came through again with his plow, he'd throw dirt up on the seeds and push them further back between the stalks. The pea vine fertilized the ground; the corn provided climbing stakes for the peas and we would have a crop of peas or beans in the field at frost. Our timing had to be right. Vines grow faster than corn, so we had to let the corn get a good head start or it would get strangled before it matured. Of course we had to pick the beans and peas before we could get to the corn, but that was all right. The corn needed to stand there for a while to get completely dry before we harvested it or it would mold when we put it in the barn.

Papa also grew red velvet beans among the cornstalks. He would add them to the bushels of corn he took to the feed mill where they'd run it all through a grinder. The beans would enrich the feed, and you could tell when we had fed it to the cows—the milk was richer and the butter was a lot heavier. But those beans were so fuzzy, I can't think of anything fuzzy enough to compare them to. They would eat you alive when you picked them. We didn't have work gloves—didn't know they existed. When we got through picking red velvet beans we always wanted to head for the branch to take a bath.

Just about everything we grew, except cotton, went to feed the family and our animals. Little cash came in or left the Whitson farm. We did need money to buy school supplies and shoes, though, and one way we got it was to sell pulpwood off our land. We called it paper wood. Papa and Uncle Edward would go across the property and select trees to be cut. There were a lot of big sweetgums in the bottoms that were only good for paper wood. The men would hook the logs up to the mules and pull them to the banks alongside the road, then after school Karrold and I would cut them to size and remove limbs with a crosscut saw. I was ten, Karrold was six, but we were able to work that six-foot-long, double-handled saw pretty well. The sawmill wouldn't buy the sweetgums with any bark on them, so we had to peel it off. Papa went to his forge and made us some debarkers out of iron rods by hammering the ends into something like a pry bar. We'd straddle a log and peel the bark off the tree with papa's tool. It took about a week to debark a load of that sweetgum wood. Then the men loaded it on Daddy's truck and hauled it off to Berry where it was piled onto a freight train heading for Tuscaloosa or Columbus, Mississippi. I don't remember if sweet-gum had a higher price than the pine wood or if Papa just wanted it out of his pasture, but anyway it was a pretty good job for Karrold and I. The rest of them weren't big enough to do it, except Esta, who chose to stay home and help my grandmother take care of the little ones. I thought doing paper wood was better because it was along-side the creek and every now and then Papa would slip the fishing poles out and we'd get a little fishing in while we were debarking the wood. If you stayed with Mama there was no chance for fun. 🐦

Know-how

Julia Whitson knew what Christian duty was and she did it. She fed and clothed us, saw that we slept warm at night and tended to our illnesses and injuries.

With the help of her two daughters, Ezzie and Lois, she made most of our clothes, even our underwear. The fabric came from fertilizer sacks, feed sacks and flour sacks. Each sack was nothing more than one big rectangle of fabric folded over and stitched along the side and at one end. The other end would be stitched shut after the sack was filled. When we had used whatever was in a sack, we would pull the stitches out and turn it back into a big piece of cloth. We saved the thread—we called it raveling thread—for other projects like crocheting doilies or making homemade baseballs.

The fabric from fertilizer sacks—of course, we called them gu-anner sacks—was thick and a bit rough but would do for underwear. Feed sacks were nicer and flour sacks were the best. If we had white flour sacks we used them to strain milk or we turned them into embroidered pillowcases and dresser scarves. Flour and feed sacks that were printed with flowers or polka dots or stripes became our dresses. Mama could make a dress for any of the three girls out of two or three printed sacks. If she only had one sack in a certain pattern and Papa was going to the store to buy feed, she'd say, "Now I need one or two more sacks like this and I can make so and so a dress," and he would try to find that pattern. If he brought home a checked pattern or a solid color, as long as it wasn't pink or some other girlish color, she'd make Karrold or Milford a shirt.

We had very plain, small wardrobes because of the way we did our laundry. We didn't have a washing machine when we first moved there. We hauled everything down to the wash place on the branch, scrubbed it on a rub board, washed it in a big pot of boiling water, wrung it out by hand and hung it out on the clothsline. Doing laundry for three adults and five children—school clothes, heavy work clothes, washcloths, towels and linens for four beds—took all day. If we had tossed our clothes in the hamper after one wearing, we'd be doing nothing but laundry. We had our clothes that we wore to school, church, or on visits, and we had our work clothes that were not presentable enough to be worn in public. After we had done our chores in the morning, we would get dressed in our school clothes and change out of them as soon as we came home in the afternoon. After one wearing, we'd put our clothes back on a hanger to be worn another time or two.

Our house was heated by only one fireplace and the cook stove and in order to stay warm at night we needed a pile of quilts on each bed. Because she saved all the scraps of fabric left over when she made our clothes and because we collected so many feed and fertilizer sacks during the year, there were abundant materials around the house for quilting. Mama's quilting needles came from the insurance man; every Liberty National Insurance agent worth his salt brought needles to his customers. Except for balls of thread we bought, our quilts were made from things we already had on hand.

Mainly Mama made strip-pieced quilts. I don't remember her ever cutting out very many quilt pieces; she just put together the scraps she had regardless of their shape, size, or texture. Thick wool, denim, and khaki scraps went side by side with scraps from our summer cotton dresses. She used pages torn from the Sears, Roebuck catalog as a base for the patchwork to give it strength and shape. To do that she would put two scraps of material with the right sides facing and sew them to each other and to the paper at the same time. Then she would open the pieces up so that the pretty sides were facing out, put another piece face down on the last scrap she had attached, sew it the same way, then flip it open—on and on until the page was covered with patchwork. She would trim off any scraps that stuck out beyond the edge of the page, then tear another page from the catalog and start over again. When she'd done four pages, she would join them into one block and when she had twenty blocks, she would cut feed sacks into long, narrow strips and sew them to the blocks. The strips were the grids that connected the patchwork squares and turned them into a quilt top.

She used gu-anner sacks for the backing or lining of the quilt. After she had unraveled the sides of the sacks and washed them, she would sew them together to make a piece the size of the quilt top, then she would dye that piece brown or dark blue using walnut hulls or pokeberries.

The stuffing for the quilt came from our cotton field. At night Mama would sit by the fire with a big wooden comb turning clumps of cotton into long, thin strands. She put these into a box and when she had enough for a quilt, she would lower the quilt frame from where it hung close to the ceiling. She attached the quilt bottom to the frame and covered it with a layer of cotton maybe a quarter-inch thick. Then she carefully covered that with the patchwork quilt top. After she loosely basted the top, stuffing, and bottom together, she began to quilt. Quilting had no purpose other than to hold the three layers together through many winter nights and through many hours of being sloshed in the washpot and hung on the clothesline. Even though Mama didn't intend for the stitches to be decorative, she still made them small and uniform and sewed them in what quilters call the shell pattern, which really looks more like rainbows than shells.

Believing that idle hands are the devil's workshop, Mama involved us in quilting during the winter months when we couldn't work in the fields. I had a little box that I kept my sewing in, and any time during the daylight hours other than Sunday—we didn't work on quilts or anything else on Sunday—she would have me get it out after my regular chores were done. I remember that I pieced my first quilt top when I was nine. During Christmas vacation that year, we set up the quilting frame in the room where the fireplace was and Esta and I began quilting it. The cotton batting had lumps in it and our thread was coarse, but Mama expected us to make fine stitches anyway. To her, needlework said something about your integrity— the finer your needlework, the finer your character. She was talented at it and she expected everybody else to have that knack, whether they did or not. She stood over us while we quilted and if she saw any lumps, puckers, or crooked corners where the squares met, we took them out and did that section over and over until she was satisfied. I was sure I would never quilt again when I got on my own.

Mama also knew how to keep us well or cure us when we weren't. In the years we lived with her I don't remember any of us going to the doctor. The only medicines we had were those she made. She gathered yellow root that grew by the branch below the house, boiled it down to a concentrate and blended it with lard. We used that yellow root salve for redbug bites and any nicks and cuts we got. She gave us blackberry juice for diarrhea and upset stomachs, and made teas and salves out of plants with names like Indian Turnip, Queen of the Meadow, and tread salve. She made cough medicine out of rock candy and whiskey—that was the only time she ever allowed any alcohol in the house—and rubbed our chests with a homemade camphor salve. In the springtime I'd have chills and run a temperature—Papa called it spring fever—and she would treat it with quinine.

Mama also was our emergency-room physician. I still have a scar to remind me of the time I was cutting corn tops to feed the mules. To do so, I had to stretch up on my tiptoes and cut down towards myself with a long knife. I gave a hard whack to one of the stalks and whacked my forearm, putting a deep gash there. I dropped the knife and walked to the house holding my arm out to keep the blood off of my dress. Mama took kerosene, our chief disinfectant, poured it in the wound, and bandaged it up. Another time we were all below the mule barn cutting corn stalks. Some of us were chopping them down and some were picking them up and carrying them to a pile. Milford bent over to pick up stalks just as Esta's hoe was coming down to chop more. It hit the back of Milford's head and laid it open. Papa grabbed him, took him to the house, and set him in a wooden chair. Mama got the straight razor out and shaved the hair around the wound. Then she got her needle, heated it in the fireplace, bent it the way she wanted it, threaded it, and sewed Milford up. In both cases we probably couldn't have made it to town in the mule wagon to see the doctor without bleeding to death first.

I know it sounds like this was all happening some time in the nineteenth century, but we lived with Mama and Papa in the mid-to-late 40s when children in Fayette, 15 miles away, ate food from the grocery store, rode in cars with their parents to church, and went to the doctor's office when they were sick or injured. But we weren't very different from other farm families in Fayette County. Every child I knew worked. School started early in the summer and let out during the months of September and October so that we could help gather the crops. Those who didn't work on their own farms would hire out and work for other people. Black and white, we all got out there and picked cotton and pulled fodder and cut hay and made sorghum syrup and hominy and dug potatoes. Most of us lived in unpainted, unplumbed houses and wore homemade feed sack dresses and shirts and didn't think of ourselves as poor at all. ☙

Outcasts

My brothers and sisters and I were different from the rest in one way that mattered very much. My mother had left my father. It would not have been such a scandal if my father had left us. People would have offered help and sympathy. But Mother stayed right there in Berry and continued her relationship with John Hyde. Now Berry is a small place where everybody knows everybody else's business. In the 1940s divorce carried a big stigma and Mother flaunted hers by staying in town. For that reason some parents did not allow their children to play with us. All of us felt like outcasts, and I for one became so defensive that I became a bully in school. I remember when I was in the seventh grade a boy called me a S.O.B. and I punched him so hard that he fell backward over a desk and sat up with a bloody nose.

Out on the farm, we were pretty much in the dark about what Mother was doing, but we went to school in Berry where it was common knowledge that John's mother had forbidden Mother and him to live together. She said that if she ever found them in bed, she would kill them. John took her at her word and did not marry Mother until after Mrs. Hyde died. However he moved a two-room shanty onto some property he owned and fixed it up for her to live in. It was really more like a tool shed than a house, and that was where our mother—who had once had a hard-working husband, five children, nice furniture and a car—was living. After she left Daddy, she made no attempt to communicate with any of us children and it was not until years later that Aunt Ezzie told us what Mother thought about the situation.

It broke Aunt Ezzie's heart, she said, to think of five children's home being torn up and of our being treated so severely by our grandmother, who was old and tired and cross with us. So Ezzie went to my mother and begged her to go back to her real husband. Mother said she couldn't stand being married to him anymore, so

Ezzie said, "Why don't you two see after your children even if you are divorced?" Mother told her that she had wanted to do that but Daddy had refused. If they couldn't be man and wife, he said, he didn't want her to have anything to do with raising the children. She was as stubborn as he was and decided to have nothing at all to do with us. Later, though, she came to Ezzie, Daddy's favorite sister, and asked her to help get some—not all—of the children back. Ezzie said she wouldn't be part of separating the children that way, so Mother went out to the farm to talk to Mama about it.

I remember seeing Mother briefly before I was sent away to do something. All I know is that some screaming and yelling took place and all of us remained with Mama and Papa. Ezzie would not tell us which of the children Mother wanted, but I know that it was Esta and Karrold. They were most like her; the rest of us favored Daddy and we knew that she called us "Bradley's little S.O.B's."

It's true that Esta took after Mother. She looked like her and had her ways. She was probably as miserable as I was at Mama and Papa's, but she was cunning and devised ways to keep herself out of trouble. I took a lot of very hard whippings because of her. For instance, we had to wash dishes together everyday. We didn't have a sink so we washed off the end of the table in dishpans. It was my job to wash the dishes in soapy water and then pour rinse water over them. Esta would dry them and put them away. We didn't dare get a drop of water on Mama's floor, which had to be polished by hand.

One night I was washing out a gallon jar. My hand would not fit down into it. So I put some dishwater in it and dropped the dishrag into it and swashed it around. Suddenly Esta reached up and slapped it out of my hand. The milk jug slid the length of the table and down onto Mama's precious floor. When Mama stormed in the room to see what had happened, Esta told her I was fooling around and dropped it. I'll never forget the beating I took for that.

She did such things constantly. The incident that bothered me most occurred when I was about 11 and she was nine. By this time Mama had an electric washing machine. Her sons had cut timber off of the place and sold it in order to buy her a wringer washer. However, we still didn't have running water so we would tote water up from the branch the evening before and put it in tubs where she could dip the clean water into the washer and throw the dregs on the flowers.

Down at the branch Papa had dug steps in the bank where we could stand to dip our buckets. This particular time Esta noticed that if you spilt a little bit of water on the steps, you could slide on them and that was fun. It was in the summertime and we were all barefooted. She poured a little more water out and in the ensuing sliding, she fell in the branch and muddied the water. Right away she realized she was going to be in trouble. In order to save her own hide, she dropped her buckets and ran wet and muddy back to the house, yelling that I had pushed her in. I wasn't even there when she fell in. I was going back down to get another bucket of water. My brothers told Mama that I didn't push Esta in, but she didn't believe them. All that mattered to her was that the branch was muddy and we would have to wait for the water to settle. She whipped me until blood ran down my legs then made me tote the rest of the wash water myself. I have no idea how many trips I had to make up and down that hill the rest of the day until the boys decided to help me. I reckon they felt sorry for me.

And I felt sorry for myself. No one—except two younger brothers—cared whether I had been falsely accused or cared whether I was happy or miserable. No one told me I was smart, good, talented, or pretty. Real mothers believe in the beauty and worth of their children and take their side against the world, if need be, but I didn't have a real mother. And Daddy didn't understand anything about his children's need for love and emotional support and never stayed home long enough to give it. It was about this time that I started thinking about the kind of mother I would be and the kind of home I would have someday. I resolved that I would give my children the things I dreamed of myself. I didn't think about finishing school and having a career, I just thought about having a good husband and raising a houseful of happy children. I thought about what I would fix them for supper and the presents I would give them on their birthdays. As I went about my chores for Mama and Papa I imagined I was a mother doing them for her own sweet family. 🐦

Play

Three words I never heard Mama say: "Y'all go play." When we finished our chores she'd have us piecing a quilt or she'd give us a square of fabric with a hole cut in it and make us practice finishing it off with a buttonhole stitch. But we did manage to eke out a little time to play—mainly because Mama didn't believe in working on Sunday. Even though she was extremely religious, Mama didn't go to church. I don't know if it was because she was anti-social or if she couldn't spare the time. Still, she allowed no work on the Sabbath other than cooking Sunday dinner, feeding the animals, and bringing in wood and water.

Often some of her children would come visit on Sunday, bringing us cousins to play with. After dinner we'd go over the hill, out of earshot, and not come back to the house for any reason, even for supper. If we did, Mama was sure to find some little task or errand for us to do. Beyond the sound of her voice we would build pine-straw playhouses and rest on pine-straw beds. We played baseball with a stick bat and a ball made from a cork wrapped in raveling thread. When the boys got bigger they played a fierce game where they would get on one side of the pine thicket and see who could reach the other side first by swinging from tree to tree. Even Daddy participated in that game. Each one would climb to the top of the tree, make it start swaying, then swing over and grab another tree. If the top of the tree broke, down they'd go—thirty or forty feet. They didn't kill themselves because they were tough and wiry and the tree branches would break their fall.

The only other chance we had to play was in the summer when there would be a little time between sundown and dark. Maybe an uncle would come by with one or two of his children. The grownups would sit on the porch and talk while we played kick the can or hide-and-go-seek. And there would be evenings in the wintertime when we'd bake sweet potatoes in the fireplace or pop popcorn on an open fire and tell stories while we ate it. Mama sometimes told about her family, the Kimbrells. Her father died when she was seven and her mother died when she was 11, so she was passed around amongst her relatives while she was growing up. According to her, they were mean people. Our great-grandfather Kimbrell killed his son-in-law and died in jail. From such stories I could see that Mama came by her meanness honestly. I never imagined that in a few years I would become a double-dip Kimbrell.

One event we looked forward to in late summer was syrup-making time. There were two or three sorghum makers in the area with portable mills. One would come into our community bringing sorghum pans, a mule-drawn press, and everything needed to make syrup. In exchange for the use of his equipment, he would take a percentage of each farmer's syrup. Usually the women stayed home and tended to their chores and the men came prepared to spend the day. One would be in charge of the fire, another would feed sorghum stalks into the mill, one made sure the mule kept turning the press, and everyone took turns cutting wood for the fire. A farmer would make his syrup one day and then help the others make theirs the next. The sorghum making was held close to Mama and Papa's farm and we went there every chance we got. With the neighbor children we'd throw sticks in the fire, sneak tastes of the syrup, and watch the mule walk round and round turning the press. By the time everyone's syrup was made, that poor old mule had a good deep circle carved into the ground.

But the best social event for us was Decoration Day. Each church had a day when folks would gather to decorate graves in the cemetery. On the fourth Sunday in April every year we went to the decoration at Cedar Grove, a little church a mile and a half from Mama and Papa's. That's where Daddy's people are buried. Some families made a practice of going to a lot of decorations, but we only went to this one because we didn't have transportation to get to most of them.

On Decoration Day we honored the memory of our deceased by

maintaining and beautifying their graves. We made our own artificial flowers out of red crepe paper with baling wire stems. We'd make the petals by curling the edges of the paper with a table knife, the way you curl ribbons. When we stretched the paper, the edges would cup over and look like a real rose petal. Some people dipped them in paraffin to get them through at least the first rain. We also brought live flowers in jars and cans. Mama always had some flowers in bloom that time of the year.

The graves were mounds of clean sandy soil kept clear of grass. We would stick the stems of the paper roses directly into the grave. For the live flowers, we would dig a hole in the grave, set a container of water in it and then put dirt back around it to keep it from tumping over. In it would go whatever was blooming at the time, perhaps just a bouquet of honeysuckle. There were no elaborate arrangements such as you see today. If no family members showed up to tend certain graves, others would put flowers on them and the entire cemetery would be decorated by dinnertime.

Mama always cooked chicken and dumplings for the big meal, so we had to get up even earlier than usual in order to kill the chickens, pluck and boil them, prepare the dumplings, and still get to the decoration on time. If someone had been to town or the rolling store had stocked bananas that week, Mama also made banana pudding. Banana pudding was the big delicacy in those days.

When the food was ready and the chores done, we'd put on our best clothes. I only had one Sunday dress, but I remember getting some new white sandals for Decoration Day. I was in high society—or walking in white cotton, as we said—in those new shoes. Sometimes Daddy would take us to the decoration in his log truck, but most of the time we went in the wagon. We couldn't walk because we were toting big iron pots of food and jars full of flowers. Lots of folks came in mule-drawn wagons or on horseback even though this was in the late 1940s and cars were common everywhere except among country folks.

The food was spread out on long tables under the trees. There was chicken in all forms—fried, boiled with dumplings, or baked with dressing. It was in late April and folks scrambled to serve the first and freshest English peas, carrots, and new potatoes of the season. And of course there would be a great number of cakes and fruit pies. Usually someone more affluent than the rest of us brought lemonade. It would be in a wooden barrel with a 100-pound block of ice floating in it. And you talk about something good—that was good. If I had it now, it probably wouldn't taste one-third as good as it did then. It couldn't have been much more than water with some lemon slices and a little sugar in it, but lemons were exotic fruits to us. At home we only drank water and milk, so that icy fresh lemonade was a delicacy.

Folks at the Decoration Day didn't necessarily belong to Cedar Grove church or live anywhere near it, it just happened that someone in their family was buried there. We saw people we hadn't seen since the year before, chatted about who had been born, married, or died, and noticed who had gotten taller and cuter in the last year. I wasn't interested in boys at that time, but for those who were it was a good opportunity to meet and flirt with boys from other communities, even though they might be distant relatives.

The rolling store provided another break in our routine and isolation. On Tuesday mornings Mr. Christian would drive up in his tall panel truck, park, go around to the back, and lower a set of stairs that led up to shelves full of groceries. Most of the time Mama stood on the ground and told him what she wanted, but sometimes we would get to go in and admire his stock, particularly the selection of candy bars he kept near the door. Mama never bought us any, but sometimes she would buy cocoa or coconut or bananas and vanilla wafers to make us something sweet. She didn't pay cash for anything—she traded fresh butter, vegetables from the garden, eggs, and live chickens for the few things that she and Papa didn't grow themselves, such as coffee and snuff. Mr. Christian had a coop hung from the back of his truck. He'd put one or two of Mama's chickens in it and haul them off squawking to Berry, where town folks would buy them. ❧

Butch

Mama was proud of her ability to provide the family with goods from the rolling store, mainly due to her precious chickens. They were hers and hers alone—she fed them, gathered their eggs, and chose which ones would become Sunday dinner. I guess it was bound to happen that Mama would eventually accuse our beloved Butch of crimes involving her chickens. When it did, it was the most painful episode of our four years at Mama and Papa's.

Mama didn't like Butch because he had been as undisciplined as we were when we arrived. He was used to staying inside and even sleeping with us when we lived in Berry. Mama wouldn't let him in the house, so there had been some busted out screen doors and other problems at first. One of her daughters, our Aunt Lois, had a bulldog that Mama and Papa liked. One day Aunt Lois and Uncle Robert brought the bulldog over and left him while we all went to the funeral of a neighbor. Daddy got off work and took some of us to the church in the logging truck and some of us went in Lois and Robert's car. When we returned, Mama found some torn up chickens and went on a tear. She yelled at Papa to get the gun and kill every dog. "They've killed my chickens, you kill those dogs." Daddy knew that Papa would just shoot Butch and not his own dog Boots or Aunt Lois's bulldog, so he said he'd do it. He went inside, got his gun and a biscuit. "I'll kill the first dog to pick up the first piece of bread." When he threw out the biscuit, Aunt Lois's dog ran out from under the house and Daddy killed it. Papa didn't like the way that turned out so he went in and got another biscuit and made Daddy do it again. The first dog out from under the house this time was Butch. Daddy shot and hit Butch but did not kill him. Butch took off running and I went totally out of control. I called Mama every dirty name I could think of. Even though Daddy and Papa were involved in the shooting, Mama was the one pulling their strings and I vented all my anger at her. I don't know why one of them didn't beat me to death, except I think they were beginning to realize that they had done the wrong thing. They could see how distraught all of the children were. I was the only one being ugly, but the others were broken-hearted and angry too. At the time it seemed the worst thing that had ever happened to me—worse than Mother leaving us, worse than any of Mama's punishments. Butch had been our friend for almost as long as I could remember.

Daddy hunted for Butch the rest of the day and did not find him. A couple of weeks later we kids found him in the woods. His infected bullet wound smelled terribly and he could barely move, but his tail went into full motion when he saw us. Though we knew he was nearly dead we brought him food, trying to nurse him back to life. I think Papa soon realized that not all the leftovers were going to the hogs. He followed us to the hideout and convinced us that we needed to end Butch's misery. Papa killed him—at least this time it was done out of compassion instead of anger—and we buried him and grieved over the dog who had loved us through all our troubles. 🐾

Marriage

Shortly after Calvin and I married, a traveling photographer came around and offered to take my picture and send it back to me framed. When it arrived I was disappointed with how blurry it was, but I kept it because it was the only photo of me that we had.

Suddenly we were free. I don't know what led up to it, except it was obvious that Mama and my father were not getting along. When they were starting up a fight, I would try to go out in the woods or the other side of the barn where I couldn't hear them. But I imagine Mama was coming down real hard on Daddy for staying away too much and not assuming enough responsibility for his children. I just remember Daddy storming up to me one day and telling me that we were leaving. That was perfectly fine with me.

We moved about two miles across the creek to Jesse and Donie

Sands' place, where Daddy had rented a fairly new house. It was the standard tenant farmer's house with no paint, plumbing, or sealed walls, but it was clean. We still had the furniture Daddy bought for Mother in Berry. Mama had kept it at her house while we were there, so, of course, it was in good condition. By this time I was well-grounded in preparing meals, gathering vegetables from the garden, and keeping the house clean. At 12 years old I was ready and willing to play house with Daddy and my brothers and sisters. During that time on our own I remember doing things for Daddy and thinking that one of these days I'll be doing this for me. I thought of the ideal little house, ideal little kids and ideal husband that I would have some day.

Donie Sands was kin to Papa and was nice to us. She took care of Doris, who was four, while the rest of us were in school. We didn't stay at the Sands' place very long, but in that time I bonded with Donie's daughter Nell. She was the first best friend I had. After we moved away I got to go back and spend the night with her from time to time. I enjoyed not having to cook. We washed dishes and made up beds, but those chores can be fun with a friend. On the first day I rode the bus with her to my new school in Bankston she told me "When we get a little further down the road here, there's a bunch of boys that get on the bus and I'm going to show you mine. You can have any of the others you want but don't fool with him because he's mine." Sure enough, when they finished school they got married.

Right away I could tell I would like my new school. The kids didn't know my background and seemed to accept me for myself. It was hard to take care of Daddy and the kids and go to school, but I was determined to do it.

We had only been at the Sands' place a week when Daddy went with me to the spring to tote water. I knew something was up because he never did things with me.

"I want to talk to you about something," he said, "and I don't want you to tell anybody."

I promised I wouldn't and he said, "I'm going to take y'all down to Aunt Ethel's tomorrow for the weekend." I was happy to hear that we were going to Aunt Ethel's. Even though she was my mother's sister, she and Daddy had remained on good terms. She had seven children and we loved to play with them. Then he went on to say, "I found a woman that will come in here and help take care of y'all, and I'm going to get married." I was overjoyed. I didn't ask who he was marrying but visions of a mother who would help me cook and do laundry and take care of Doris flew into my head.

All weekend at Aunt Ethel's I thought about my new mother. Would she be kind like Donie Sands? Or maybe she would be smart like Aunt Lois. Aunt Lois lived in town in a white painted house with an indoor bathroom. She had money and a car. When I spent the night there, I'd wake up in a pretty room with painted walls and hear the wrens chirping outside. It was heaven. Hopefully she would be sweet like Aunt S'phronie, who was married to one of Papa's brothers. She was a small lady with a wonderful smile. She and Uncle Jeff had a huge family—fourteen kids, I think, and lots of grandkids my age. They had the biggest dinner table I've ever seen. It sat about thirty people. Mama, who never went with us when we visited, would always say, "Now when you go up to there and eat, you have to help wash the dishes." But Aunt S'phronie would say "You just go on and play and we won't tell Aunt Julie you didn't wash dishes today."

Daddy had been spending a lot of time in Columbus—I think that's what he and Mama got into it about. I figured he had met someone there, a smart city woman who would come here and love five kids. I could hardly wait for Daddy to pick us up on Sunday so we could meet her. When he arrived with his new bride, any visions of a normal life with a lovely mother vanished. It was Clara, a neighbor girl in her 20s, that I had never liked. I did not pretend for a moment to be happy for them. The first time Daddy left the house, I threw a fit. I told her that Daddy shouldn't have married her and that she would never be my mother. And she never was.

I don't know why Daddy believed that this young woman would

be able to take care of his five children. Maybe he was thinking of her mother, who he had known since he was a child. She was meticulous. She wore her hair combed back into a neat bun and she always wore aprons—even to church. They were starched and ironed and perfectly white. She was a fine cook, and every one said that her house, like Mama's, was so clean that you could eat off her floors. But unlike Mama, she did not train her daughters to be good housekeepers. My new stepmother could not cook or clean. I ended up doing all the chores I had done before Daddy remarried. Now that I look back I understand that she was young and homesick—if I had had a wonderful mother like hers I would have been homesick too. Perhaps we would have been friends if I had been more compassionate and less belligerent. Instead we did all that we could to make each other miserable.

Clara wanted to go home to her mother's every weekend. Daddy would not let her go until the laundry was done and the house cleaned up. So she would get him to keep Esta and me out of school to help her. She was home all day with nothing to do but watch after Doris and Milford and cook dinner for Daddy, but we had to miss school and do laundry. She couldn't make me mind her, so she had to get Daddy to discipline me when I refused to do what she said. That led to the last whipping that Daddy ever gave me.

One Friday afternoon she wanted to go to her mother's but she had not done the laundry yet and knew Daddy wouldn't let her go. When we got off the school bus, she had everything ready for us to help get it done. She said I could either help do laundry or cook supper. I told her I wasn't going to do either one—I was going to find the cow. Peggy had not come up the night before to be milked and it was too late to go look for her. I thought Daddy or someone would look for her the next morning, but she wasn't in the lot when I got home, so I knew I had to do it. The man we were renting from had hundreds of acres, fenced off in different pastures. Someone had left open the gate down to the short pasture where we kept Peggy and she had gotten into the lower pasture, which was a good four or five miles from the house. When you start hunting a cow on several hundred acres with all these little knolls to go up and down over, it can take a while. So they did the laundry without me and left it up to me to cook supper. It was after dark when I found the cow and got her home and milked. By then Daddy was home from the fields and had heard the stories they concocted about me. He was angry that there was no supper on the table and proceeded to give me a big whipping. In the country, people didn't use psychological methods of punishment. Daddy couldn't send me to my room because I didn't have a room. It would have been too easy—in fact it would have been a treat—to go stand with my nose in a corner. So Daddy got a big switch and whipped the back of my legs until there were welts on it.

I was 13 now and I had pretty much made up my mind I'd had all I was going to take. I didn't cry. I told him, "You'd better whip me all you want to. If you didn't, you'd better go back and do it again, because this is the last you'll ever whip me."

By this time we had left the Sands' place and were living at George Cotton's place, where Daddy was farming and maintaining Mr. Cotton's machines. If I had not been having such a hard time with my stepmother and my sister, I would have loved living there. George Cotton was a friendly man with a laugh you could hear five miles away. He was an entrepreneur and, now that I know what a visionary is, I'd say he was one. He owned a lot of land and turned it into a resort where local folks could spend the day swimming, fishing, picnicking, and riding horses over trails he'd cleared through his woods. He put a dam on Clear Creek and used the water that flowed over it to power a gristmill that he could convert into a sawmill by changing out the belts and pulleys. Clear Creek got its name honestly and the swimming area above the dam was sparkling. On Thursday and Saturday nights Mr. Cotton showed movies outside. We got to go to those free because Daddy ran the projector.

He also built a little grocery store on his property that stocked nonperishable essentials, like flour, sugar, and tobacco. Most country people used tobacco in one form or another—hand-rolled cigarettes, cigars, or snuff—and Cotton's was the only place within 15 miles to get it.

Every five years or so Mr. Cotton would drain his pond and fry hundreds of pounds of fish he collected off the bottom. Folks would come from all over the county for the fish fry, even though they considered him curious. He just did things different than most people in Fayette County. He had hundreds of ducks in the pond and he gathered their eggs from his boat by tying a rope around Milford's waist and putting him out in the water to collect them. Later, though, most of the ducks were killed by two baby foxes he had raised himself after accidentally killing their mother. He also had big herds of goats and sheep. One spring, after the goats all dropped their litters, Mr. Cotton decided to try his hand at selling goat milk. The goats were pastured away from everything else and went six months at a time without ever seeing human beings. They were so wild that it took three people to milk each one. Daddy held the front legs, Mr. Cotton the hind legs, and Milford did the milking. After a few weeks Mr. Cotton abandoned that idea and went on to something else. But he was good to us, especially my younger brothers and sisters, and gave them some fun and attention that they didn't get at home.

Cotton's establishment was across the road from our house. Down a hill on the right was the Cleveland Church of Christ that also played a big part in our social lives. The main thing that country people like us did for entertainment was go to revivals. One night in June or July there was a revival going on and a good-looking stranger showed up at our house to see if I wanted to go to church with him. Calvin Kimbrell was some distant kin to my grandmother and Daddy had worked some with him and knew his family, but I'd never seen him before.

"I don't know. You'll have to ask Daddy."

As usual I was mad at Daddy about something and in a bad mood. I just wanted everybody to go away and leave me alone. I went ahead with my milking and when I got back in the house, Calvin was still there. Without speaking to him I went straight into the kitchen, strained the milk and put it in the refrigerator. Calvin came in and said, "I'm waiting on you to go to church."

"Did you ask Daddy?"

"Yeah. He said okay."

So I went with him to church and if you could call that a date, it was my very first date ever. Calvin was seventeen and fun to be with, so when he asked if he could come back again sometime I said yes.

I was more interested in a boy I'd met horseback riding over at Cotton's, but Calvin was persistent. He would come to see Daddy because he knew he wasn't making any headway with me. He spent afternoons with Daddy tinkering around on his machines or they'd go off fishing. He could communicate with Daddy better than me and felt like if he could get in with Daddy then he had an in with me. The more he stayed around the more I noticed how handsome he was. He was tall—about six foot four—and thin. He had beautiful black hair and a dark tan from working out in the fields. The most attractive thing about him was his enjoyment of life. He didn't dwell on serious things; he preferred to flirt and joke and laugh. But he took time to talk to people, listen to what they were saying, and help them in anyway he could. Before long he was my boyfriend and I could tell him about my conflicts with my stepmother and sister and the unjust spankings I got from my father. Calvin was firmly on my side—outraged at the way they treated me—and that was a wonderful feeling. The fact that we were something like fifth cousins didn't bother us at all.

He lived about 14 miles away and didn't have a car, but he would try to get rides over to Cotton's movie theater on Thursdays and Saturdays. There we had the whole family as chaperones, but Daddy wouldn't let us go off by ourselves because I was so young. If we wanted to go to a revival at another church, we had to go with some of our family members.

One night we were planning to go to a revival in the Possum Trot community, about 15 miles up the road. Calvin's neighbor Clarence had offered us a ride in his car. Milford and Karrold had gone to spend the night with Mama and Papa. Clara, who was five or six months pregnant, was going to stay home with Doris. That left Esta as our chaperone at the revival. That evening, however, she and I had another fight and out of spite she said she wouldn't go to church with me. When Calvin came to pick me up I went out and told him "Daddy won't let me go." He wanted to know why.

"Esta's mad at me and won't go with us."

"I'm going to go ask, anyway."

"Well, you go ask, but he's not going to let me go."

Daddy was eating when Calvin came in and told him, "Me and Clarence come and was going to go to church up at Possum Trot tonight and wanted to know if Bettye could go."

Daddy enjoyed tormenting people. He sat there without saying a word. He ate a few more bites then slowly looked around the table at all of us. He had figured out why Esta didn't want to go. Finally he asked, "Well, how long are y'all going to be gone?"

Calvin said, "We'll be back soon as church is over."

"Well, I tell you what I'm going to do. I'm going to let you go, but you have to be back no later than 9:30."

Esta sat there with an open mouth, amazed at Daddy's answer. Now that I was getting to go it was not going to be a bit fun for her to stay home. She told him she would go to church after all, but Daddy said no. That was the only time he ever took up for me.

Young people who went to church on dates usually stayed outside under a tree and talked. I decided that since Daddy trusted me to go by myself I was going to go inside to the worship service. While we were in the church, somebody let every bit of the air out of all four of Clarence's tires. That was a common prank in those days and I'm sure Clarence had played it on plenty of other folks. The only thing we had to air those tires up with was a hand pump, so by the time we got home it was way past 9:30. Daddy was home from fishing and I just knew he'd beat me to death, but he didn't. Calvin and Clarence told him what happened and I reckon he believed them.

David—Clara and Daddy's first child together—was born at our house early in October and that was the start of Daddy's second, and favorite, set of five children. About a week after his birth, a hurricane came in at Mobile and made its way up to Fayette County. Daddy had some of the prettiest corn in the field beside the house until that hurricane made spaghetti out of it. The only way to gather the corn was to get in one spot, pick up a stalk at a time, and cut off each ear. So Daddy hired Calvin, who had quit school several years back, to help him do that. The rest of us were out of school for harvest time and were picking cotton.

Calvin stayed at our house for a week and before very many evenings had passed, we decided to get married. Calvin was 17 and I was almost 14. He was the only man I had ever dated; he didn't have a job and we didn't have a place to live, but we were going to get married. We knew we had the same ideals and beliefs, and I was certain that life with Calvin would be better than with Daddy and Clara. The only problem I had with the idea of marriage was leaving my brothers and sisters. They had been my charge since before Daddy and Mother separated. As long as I could remember it had been my responsibility to take care of them. Even though I wanted to get away from my situation at home, it made me sad to think of leaving Karrold and Milford and Doris. So when Calvin said we should just run away together I said, "The only way I'll get married is if you talk to Daddy and he agrees, because I don't want to make him mad enough that he won't let me be with the kids. I have to be where I can be with them."

So Calvin asked Daddy the next day while they were chopping corn and Daddy said it was all right. He asked where we were going to live and Calvin told him that we would stay at his daddy's until we got our own place. Of course, Calvin had not consulted with his parents on this; they didn't even know me. Daddy didn't question Calvin any further. I'm sure he was thrilled that I was going off to be someone else's problem for a while.

We set the date for the following Saturday—Oct. 21, 1950—and decided to get married in Columbus, Mississippi rather than Fayette because in Alabama you had to get permission from your parents if you were under 18. In Mississippi they didn't care how old you were. Calvin and I went down the road and asked our neighbors Joe and Thelma Frost if they would take us to Columbus next Saturday to get married, and they agreed. It started raining about midweek and kept on raining, so Daddy had time to take me to Fayette to buy a dress to get married in. That was the only time that he ever bought me any clothes. We went to Sterman's Department Store and I picked out a dress made of aqua taffeta. It had a full skirt, like the poodle skirts that were so popular then. We called them circle tail skirts—if you sat on the ground in one, the material would make a complete circle around you. The dress had a fitted bodice and a silver chain in front that attached to each side of the collar. Daddy bought me a pair of white sandals to wear with it. Calvin hadn't brought anything but work clothes to our house, but he had a khaki shirt and a pair of khaki pants that were pretty new. We washed them and hung them behind the stove to dry.

Joe and Thelma drove us to the Lowndes county courthouse in Columbus early that Saturday morning. It was a tall brick building with arched windows, white columns that stretched two stories high, and an ornate clock tower topped with a dome. I was terrified, not because I was a teen bride but because I was in a strange town in a fancy courthouse, standing in front of a justice of the peace wearing a black robe, a man who seemed more educated and refined than anyone I had ever met. Calvin was happy-go-lucky as usual, cracking his jokes and generally enjoying himself. But neither of us knew what we were getting ourselves into.

Calvin had the $15 that Daddy had paid him for working that week. Out of that we paid something like $8 to the Frosts for gasoline and $3 for the marriage license. We stopped on the way back to get hamburgers and when we got home we had a dollar and

62 cents to start our married lives with.

Back at Daddy's there was no reception or no congratulations waiting for us. It was just a normal Saturday for them. They told us that Calvin's Daddy had come looking for him while we were in Columbus and left word for Calvin to come home the next day. We spent the night at Daddy's—at least they let us have a bedroom of our own for our wedding night—then headed to the Kimbrell's the next morning.

Mrs. Kimbrell was totally frustrated when she found out that her son had married a thirteen-year old girl. She had ten children. Two of her daughters were still at home and I was exactly between those two daughters in age. It seemed to her that Calvin was just bringing home another child for her to raise. In the weeks that followed she warmed up when she realized that I was not lazy or afraid to work. I felt like if I was going to be in their house, whatever chores had to be done were as much my responsibility as theirs. I was not a daughter-in-law very long before I became just one of the family. Lila, Calvin's sister just above him, says that they took me in like I belonged to them—I just fit right in. She says that they weren't going to undo what had already been done.

I can truthfully say I never had a cross word with Calvin's mother or father as long as they lived. Of course, nobody on either side of the family expected our marriage to last, but they didn't know how determined Calvin and I were. 🍃

In-laws

This is Calvin's mother and father, Andrew and Della Kimbrell, taken around 1960. They are seated in front of a pile of sawmill scraps that they used to heat their cook stove.

Calvin's daddy was Andrew Jackson Kimbrell and his mother was Della Missouri James Kimbrell. He was 58 and she was 44 when I joined the family. They were just like most of the folks in Fayette County, dirt-poor farmers, sharecroppers who never owned their own farm. It was only seven miles north of Berry, but that was a major trip for them and they made it only once a month. Lila says it was so far out in the sticks they used a hoot owl for a clock. There was nothing out there except their family, so you had to be going there to be there. You couldn't just pass by.

They never had much money, but they knew how to live off the land. Mr. Kimbrell's mother was half-Indian and it seems like he inherited a lot of Indian ways. When he wasn't farming, he was trapping. He'd trap beaver, fox and mink and trade them for the things he needed. He bred his own hunting dogs—usually Redbone or Black and Tan coonhounds—and was known for having the best. If one of his dogs was going to have a litter, folks would line up to get them. With his dogs he hunted squirrels to eat, raccoons to sell for fur, and possums he sold for meat—some people know how to cook it where it's good. Mr. Kimbrell also dug ginseng to sell and kept honey bees. He sold honey in five pound jars to folks in the area and shipped the honeycombs to a company out of St. Louis who sold them to people starting new hives.

Mr. Kimbrell was soft-spoken. He had a remarkable way of making himself heard from far away without raising his voice. If he was standing at the end of a long field and wanted to tell you something, he could speak in his normal voice and be understood. None of us ever figured out how he did that.

His wife was the daughter of a Methodist preacher who'd moved there from Cullman. She was more vocal and feisty than he was. I remember one time shortly after we married when Calvin told me he wanted something—I can't remember what it was—and I got up and gave it to him. His mama looked at me and said, " I hope you know what you are doing."

"What do you mean?"

"You know that if you do that now you're going to have it to do the rest of your life, because he's going to expect it. What you need to do is tell him to get up and get it hisself." I never did, though.

I turned 14 a month after we married. Mama and her daughters gave me a combination birthday party and wedding shower. It was the first birthday party I'd ever had; when we were kids no one gave us gifts or even said "happy birthday" to us. But on this occasion a few of my high school friends and a lot of relatives gathered. They gave us dishes, flatware, kitchen utensils, linens, and the like, and Mama gave me a quilt. She hadn't made it in honor of our wedding; it was just one of the plain quilts she made each winter, but I knew that it was not an easy gift for her to give and I felt honored to receive it. Now Calvin and I had enough to start housekeeping with, but no house. We couldn't pay rent and had to move around between Calvin's parents', his sisters', and my Daddy's houses that first winter. During that time I got pregnant and Calvin turned 18. By law he was required to register for the draft and when he told the registrar that he was married and expecting a baby, they sent him home for his marriage certificate. The war in Korea had begun and several young men from Fayette County had died there, so we were relieved when Calvin was exempted. We were not so fortunate 18 years later when the child I was carrying was drafted to serve in Vietnam.

With a child on its way, we really needed to find a place of our own. Early the next spring we found it. Clive Smith had a good-sized farm across the river from the Kimbrell's. He and Mrs. Smith had gotten to an age where they couldn't farm it by themselves and Mr. Smith offered Calvin a house and $20 a week to work there. He'd also give us milk and eggs and vegetables from their garden. Calvin accepted and we moved into our first house together. Daddy gave us a bed and a dresser and Calvin went to Berry and bought a brand new wood stove, a table, and four chairs on credit at Cannon's store. Even though the Cannons knew us, they made Daddy sign for us because we were so young.

Our new home was like all the others—unsealed walls, no plumbing, no heat. Our water came from a spring down the hill from the house and our bathroom was an outhouse. For kitchen cabinets we nailed orange crates to the wall and I made curtains for them out of feed sacks. There was an electric light hanging down in the center of each room, but no outlets for appliances, which we didn't have anyway. There were no screens on the windows. Flies and mosquitoes weren't much of a problem, but the gnats were bad and we had to make gnat smoke in the evening. We would fill a dishpan with green wood chips, start a little fire in it, and set the pan in the yard where the smoke would blow over us. We'd sleep at night with the doors open, the windows up and didn't think anything about it. It never crossed my mind that a snake—or something worse—might come in the window. A lot of things that we guard against now were not a concern at that time.

Life was pleasant at the Smiths. They went to town on Fridays and would take my shopping list and bring back what I needed. Also I could get things from the rolling store. But mainly we got our food directly from the farm—fresh milk and eggs everyday, fresh vegetables from the garden or from jars that I'd helped Daddy's family or the Kimbrells put up. We ate lots of fish that Calvin and I caught—fishing was our pastime—and if we wanted meat, Calvin would go out and kill two or three squirrels or a rabbit. In the springtime, Mrs. Smith had a yard full of chickens and she would give us one from time to time. When she gave us a chicken, we had to clean, cook, and eat it that day because we didn't have a refrigerator to stick it in.

I was sick a lot with my pregnancy, but I enjoyed married life. Calvin would go to the field in the morning and plow until dinnertime. The Smiths had a tractor, so he didn't have to work with mules there. He'd come home at noon and I'd have something cooked for him. In the summertime we might just have green beans, cornbread, a piece of onion and a tomato, with a glass of milk. We didn't have ice tea because we didn't have a freezer and we didn't have money for tea. I'd keep the milk cold by leaving it at Mrs. Smith's until dinnertime or keeping it in the spring.

Often I would go with Calvin to the fields after dinner. I had cooked enough food that we could have it again for supper, and that freed me to go fishing or berry picking since I was too pregnant to work. I'd ride on the tractor with Calvin five or six miles to the bottomlands where most of the farming was done. There was a little creek that ran down through there, and a lot of crickets were turned up by the plow that I would collect for bait. I would sit on a bank and fish while Calvin plowed. If I caught anything big enough to eat, we would have fried fish for supper with gravy and biscuits. In the summertime there were blackberries, wild huckleberries and mulberries in the woods to pick and make into jelly. The best berries were at the edge of the field. One afternoon while I was wading around in a briar thicket gathering berries, I stepped into a wasp nest and got five or six stings on my face. I did what Mama had taught me. I broke some leaves off a cocklebur plant and swabbed my face with them to take out the swelling, then I went on with my berry picking and forgot all about the green stuff on my face. Later when I went back to meet Calvin, he jumped off the tractor with the motor still running and ran to me. He thought that a snake had gotten me and I had turned green.

Of course, we had Doris and Milford and Karrold over a lot. The school bus ran right by our house and many afternoons the boys would get off and stay with us for a day or two. Calvin didn't mind; when he got me he knew my brothers and sisters were part of the package. He liked children and had the ability to converse with a child as if it was an adult. Doris hadn't even started school when we married and she stayed with us as much as possible. She was love-starved; she got no affection at home. She thought that Calvin was God's gift to the world because he'd tease her and buy gum and little knickknacks for her that she had never had before. When she spent the night at our house she crawled in our bed and told the others, "I'm going to sleep with my sister and you can go somewhere else." I wasn't about to tell her any different. Calvin would take Karrold and Milford hunting and fishing with him and if any of them happened to be with us when we were going to Calvin's parents for the weekend, they would go with us. Mrs. Kimbrell would just make another pallet on the floor.

Visiting kinfolk was our main entertainment in those days. We'd work all week and then pack up and spend the night with Mr. and Mrs. Kimbrell, or one of Calvin's brothers or sisters or with Daddy. There was always a big crowd at the Kimbrells; it was like cooking for an army. Just about all of their ten children would come home for some part of the weekend, and there might be twenty or thirty, including sons and daughters-in-law and grandchildren, there at one time.

Now Calvin's daddy was a quiet person and didn't like for anyone to talk at the dinner table; when his children did, he would scold and sometimes slap them. By the time he had a pack of grandchildren, Mr. Kimbrell just avoided the noise by not going to the table. He'd say, "Gal"—He always called Mrs. Kimbrell "Gal"—"You go ahead and feed all the kids and then I'll eat." But he enjoyed having the whole family there.

The men would spend the weekend helping their daddy with some project that needed doing, or going hunting or fishing, tossing horseshoes, shooting sling shots, and playing pranks on each other. All the Kimbrell men were outdoorsmen, but Calvin was the most dedicated. He'd go all summer long without a shirt or shoes. He could go through a briar patch barefooted. Lila says he'd get so tan that if you saw him from a distance you'd think he was wearing a brown shirt. Often he would stay out all night wading creeks and gigging fish. He'd feel up the banks of rivers and grab catfish with his hands.

The women would do a lot of cooking for that big bunch, take care of babies and talk. There were lots of stories to tell. Lila told about the night a copperhead snake poked its head up through a hole in the kitchen floor and crawled up under the bench near her brother Arnold. Their dad told him not to move and he killed it with a stick. She said a stick was his number one weapon.

They talked about walking to the one-room school house at Pea Ridge, carrying their lunches in four pound lard buckets. Some rough boys started picking on them and one of them knocked Calvin into the ditch. His brothers each grabbed one of the boys and held them down while Calvin swung his lard bucket at the one who pushed him and broke his tooth. We always laughed when someone would add, "And they didn't bother the Kimbrell family after that."

And they told about the time that all the students at Pea Ridge were being vaccinated. One of their cousins was so afraid of shots that he climbed out the window, went to the outhouse, climbed down in the hole, and hung on so the teacher couldn't get near him.

There was a lot of music in the family. Calvin's mother played guitar and mouth harp and could sing tenor and alto. She could pick the guitar Spanish style. She didn't strum; she'd chord and pick the melody. His dad could strum on a guitar and he loved to play the banjo when he could borrow one, but didn't own one himself. Just about all of the kids could play guitar and most of them went to singing schools in the summer and learned to sing four part harmony by reading shape notes. And they listened to the battery radio and memorized songs by the Chuck Wagon Gang and the Speer Family. Calvin's sisters Lila, Joycelyn, and Mavis were in a trio that sang at churches and on the radio in Fayette and Carrollton. When we got together at the Kimbrells, they would always sing and Calvin would play guitar for them. ❧

There was usually a crowd at the Kimbrell house on any weekend though this was probably a special celebration.

Birth

So I was enjoying life but I wasn't having an easy time with my pregnancy. To look at me now you'd never know it, but I was a skinny thing when I was 14. I had always had hard periods and stayed anemic most of the time. Still I planned on having Danny at home. Dr. Scrivner over in Berry would deliver children at home and that's where most women chose to have theirs, mainly to save the expense of the hospital. I had been going for regular checkups and everything seemed to be all right until the last half of the eighth month, when I started to swell and have kidney problems. Dr. Scrivner was old enough then that not very much rattled his cage. He gave me medicine that was supposed to take care of it. Calvin's mother watched over me as best she could and a couple of weeks before Danny was due to be born, Lila asked us to stay with her. She didn't want us by ourselves at the Smiths where we didn't have a car. So we stored what little we owned in an extra room at her house and moved in.

One Sunday night I felt more miserable than I had ever felt it my life. It was September and very hot. I got up to use the pot—Lila didn't have a bathroom either—and I went into convulsions. Calvin's brother drove off to call the doctor and get Daddy. I remember waking up about daylight. I could hear the rooster crowing, and as I started to become coherent, I could hear Daddy talking,

"What's Daddy doing here?" I asked, then passed out again. When Dr. Scrivner arrived he told them to get me to the hospital; I had toxemia and might not live. Somebody drove me to the hospital in Berry where I stayed five days before Danny was born. During that time Mother—the one who had left me—came to the hospital. I don't remember all of her visit because even at that point I was drifting in and out of consciousness. But she came in, told Calvin he should get the hell out of our lives, and told me "Just as soon as you have this baby I'm coming to get you. I'm going to take you home with me and I'm going to take care of you."

Calvin said, "Like hell you are." So the first visit I'd had from my mother since I was eight years old was no happy reunion. I was glad Calvin set her straight, though.

When they had my blood pressure down and got rid of most of my kidney poison, they gave me a saddle block, which was the new type of anesthetic at the time, and induced labor. Danny Kimbrell was born three weeks early, on September 26, 1951. Calvin named him after his favorite song, "Danny Boy," and gave him his own middle name, Junior. From that day forward I was the worst mother hen you've ever seen. I wouldn't let anyone take care of him but me.

After Danny was born we lived here and there, never far from Daddy or the Kimbrells, and did whatever we could to make money. Calvin farmed and made $20 a week. I picked cotton at $2 for a hundred pounds and, believe me, I never picked more than 200 pounds a day trying my hardest. Calvin took on extra work as a logger and then in the sawmills. For a while he even worked in the box factory with Mother, and the two did not get along.

During that time church revivals were still our main social outings after we married. One night when Danny was close to a year old, we went to one at Bevan Chapel, a little Missionary Baptist church founded by Brother Wiley Bevan. There was nothing out of the ordinary at the service, but somehow I felt miserable. I don't know if there are English words to explain it. Something was tugging at me and whispering that until I committed myself to the Lord and whatever his will was, I would find no peace. When Brother Bevan made the altar call I had no choice but to answer. I knew Calvin's family would laugh at me because they loved to talk about another daughter-in-law who would raise hell one week and be born again the next, but I was sincere in my conversion.

Later that summer I was baptized in a pond, actually it was an old quarry, along with seven or eight other people. The baptism was only a public sign of the fact that my life had already been changed. The altar call at Bevan Chapel was the turning point in my life. Until then I still had some of the meanness in me that I had developed to get myself through childhood. Faith replaced that meanness that night and I've never lost that feeling. It's the only thing that's kept me sane and got me through the difficult times that were still to come. ❧

Chicago

After Calvin moved to find work in Chicago, Danny and I joined him there. This was taken in our apartment in 1954.

We were having trouble making enough money to live off of and still pay our hospital bills. It had gotten to the point that farming was not profitable. The box factories and some of the sawmills had closed. It seemed like the only people in Fayette County with money were the bootleggers. A few of Calvin's brothers and sisters had already left home for Detroit to work in the auto industry and some were working at factories in Chicago. Since there was not enough work available for us to even exist, Calvin decided to go to work in Chicago and stay with his brother Melvin and his family. In the fall of 1953 he moved Danny and me in with his mother and father and left for Chicago. I was heartbroken because Calvin was another world away.

Calvin got a job working with his brother at Joslyn Manufacturing, a company that made parts for streetlights. He lived with Melvin, his wife Francis and their year-old son Ronnie in an apartment on Halsted Street on the south side of Chicago. They bought winter coats just alike and people thought they were twins. When Calvin got paid, he'd pay Melvin and Francis for his share of the rent and food, keep out some spending money for himself and send me the rest. Out of that I paid our hospital bills, saved some, and put a little aside for train fare to Chicago. I didn't tell Calvin that I was planning to join him in Chicago because I knew he'd tell me not to. He didn't intend to stay there and he liked the idea of me being at home with his parents. But I was determined to be with Calvin and after Christmas I bought my train ticket and arranged for one of Calvin's brothers to take Danny and me to Jasper to catch the train. At the first of the week I wrote to Calvin and said, "Danny and I are leaving here this Saturday and we'll be at the train station in Chicago on Sunday at such and such a time. Come pick us up."

As soon as we stepped off the train I was overwhelmed by the big city with all its rumbles and roars and rushing people. Calvin rented us a little efficiency apartment above a store, down the hall from his brother. So in 1954 at age 18 I had indoor plumbing for the first time. Our apartment had its own bathroom, a kitchen sink with one cabinet above it, a little cook top stove with a refrigerator underneath it, a sofa that made out into a bed, a chest of drawers, a table, and two chairs.

Danny and I got there in February and it snowed most of the time that we were there, so while the men were at work Francis and I mainly took turns visiting each other's apartments and watching our sons play. When we could get out we sometimes would walk down to Filene's bargain basement. Now that was big stuff when Cannon's Mercantile in Berry was the biggest place we'd shopped up until then. Of course, they didn't have some of the things we wanted to buy—cornmeal and grits, for example. If you asked northerners where to buy cornmeal, they'd laugh at you like you didn't have any sense, but if you cooked them some cornbread, they'd sure eat it.

Melvin and Calvin hated walking to work. The snow was so thick they couldn't tell where the sidewalks were and every time they turned a corner the wind would hit them in the face; it just whooped around between the buildings. Sometimes they'd reach up and feel their ears to see if they were still there. Also there were a lot of Hispanics there—whole buildings of them. Calvin said that when you walked by them you couldn't tell if they were cussing you or not.

On weekends we'd get out and walk to the park. We didn't explore a lot because we weren't secure in where we were going. Being country folks in that big city, we didn't venture a long way from where we were. If we socialized at all it was with other southerners, but for the most part we just did things with Melvin and Francis and Ronnie.

I spent a lot of time thinking about my little brothers and Doris at home. It was like I had left part of myself back there. From my earliest childhood memories, I was always the mother figure in their lives. Even when Mother and Daddy lived together, the children had depended on me to make decisions and lead the way. At school, I was the one who looked after them, like when we were going to school in Bankston right after Daddy and Clara got married. Milford was in first grade. A little boy threw a rock at him and it laid the back of his head open. Instead of trying to go find Daddy or some adult to take Milford to the hospital, the principal got me out of my classroom to ride with Milford to the doctor in Berry. He put me in the backseat, laid Milford face down on my lap and gave me a towel to hold on his head. When we got there the doctor pulled that wound apart, swabbed it out with Mercurochrome, and sewed his head up, without any kind of anesthetic. Milford didn't cry and scream. Like the rest of us, he had been battered so much that he was tough. When the doctor was finished, we rode back to the school and went home on the school bus that evening. Sitting in my apartment in Chicago I wondered who would hold my sisters' and brothers' heads or hands next time one was hurt.

I was especially worried about them now that Daddy had a

second family. The first two of the five children he had with his second wife were now living at Daddy's with four from his first family. Esta was 14, Doris had just turned nine, and the boys were in-between. Clara was overwhelmed with the responsibility of caring for six children, and Daddy didn't seem to notice or care. To avoid washing huge piles of clothes she made the children wear one outfit all week before putting it in the laundry. To minimize cooking she wouldn't let them have anything to eat when they came home starving after school. She and Daddy ignored their birthdays and didn't get them anything for Christmas, but she always had presents for her children. Fortunately, at that time Daddy was farming on Monroe and Gay Beard's place. The Beards had one grown child and when our brood moved into one of their tenant houses, Gay was happy to mother them. She saw how the older children were treated and would slip them money for lunch or a movie now and then. The kids wouldn't tell their stepmother about the money for fear she would take it away, like she did Doris' candy.

Calvin was there when that happened. Daddy was going to Berry for something and Doris asked him to bring her some candy. Now Daddy did have a soft spot for Doris—she was the only one of our set that he would do things for—so he bought her a sackful of peppermints and handed it to Clara when he got home. Later on that day, Daddy and Calvin were outside in the yard when Doris came up and said, "Did you get me any candy?"

Daddy said, "I sure did." He called Clara and asked her what she did with the candy.

"Well I put it up for David and Trisha."

Daddy told her to bring the candy out there and when she refused he cussed at her. She ended the argument by throwing it out in the yard. The dogs got it before Doris did.

Another time, right after Calvin and I got married, Milford came to our house covered in stripes from a beating. Clara's brother-in-law, who was ungodly mean to his own children, had gotten hold of Milford. I went over there and flew into a rage. "You can beat your kids all you want to," I told him, "but you lay your hands on one of these again and I'll kill you." And I think that right then I would have killed him if I'd had something to kill him with. Remembering these things made me frantic to get home.

After I'd been in Chicago six months and Calvin had been there nine, we'd had all of city life we could take. We had paid off our hospital bill and had been sending money home to Calvin's daddy to save for us. Calvin had been talking to his boss at work about wanting to come home. Now Calvin could talk to anyone and his boss really liked him. He said that Joslyn was starting a plant in Birmingham. It wasn't finished yet, but he told Calvin, "If you'll stay with me until the plant in Birmingham becomes operational, I'll transfer you there if you want to go home."

When the time came, Calvin's boss wrote him a transfer and we boarded the train for Alabama. I know one thing—I surely was glad when that train stopped in Jasper. If Daddy hadn't been there to pick us up, I would have got down on my knees and crawled all 30 miles to Berry.

Calvin's job was waiting for him in Birmingham, about three hours away from Berry. I wanted to spend time with my brothers and sisters, so we decided that Danny and I would stay at Daddy's for a while before moving to Birmingham.

With the money we'd saved up in Chicago we bought a 1947 Chevrolet Coupe. Calvin didn't feel confident driving in Birmingham, so he rode the bus. Every Sunday afternoon Daddy and I would take him to the Miss-Ala bus station in Berry—later it became Trailways—and he'd ride to downtown Birmingham and stay at the YMCA. Each day during the week some of the guys that he worked with at Joslyn would pick him up and carry him to the plant on Vanderbilt Road. I was happy at home, working in the fields with my brothers and sisters, taking care of Danny, and looking forward to Friday night when we'd pick Calvin up at the bus station and head over to the Kimbrells for a big family gathering. ✺

Daddy is holding Patricia, his first daughter with Clara, in front of the tenant house on Gay and Monroe Beard's place in 1954. My brothers and sisters lived there with Daddy's second family.

Polio

In this 1954 photo my brother Karrold is behind Daddy and Clara who are holding their son David and daughter Patricia. Milford and Doris are on the front row. Shortly after this was taken, Doris was stricken with polio.

Whenever Calvin came home, Doris would run to him and give him a big hug. She was now a sassy nine-year-old who loved to tease and flirt and argue with him. She worshipped Calvin and he considered her as much our child as Danny was. One Saturday in early June, shortly after we'd come back from Chicago, Doris went fishing with us. The wild plums were starting to ripen and we all ate some. That night Doris got sick and remained weak and nauseated all the next day. We blamed the plums. Sunday night, after we took Calvin to the bus station, Danny and I got in bed with Doris because she was crying for me. All night she burned with fever. I gave her water to drink and helped her use the bedpan whenever diarrhea struck.

The next morning I got up and fixed breakfast for Daddy before he went out to plow cotton. Doris didn't wake up right away and when I decided to wake her, she didn't respond. Finally she roused herself enough to tell me she needed to pee. When I tried to put her on the bedpan, I realized that she couldn't stand. She couldn't lift her arms. She was completely lifeless.

I sent one of the other kids over to the Beards to ask them to call the doctor and tell him that Doris was real sick. I put her back her in bed, put cold rags on her and tried to keep her comfortable, but she remained totally limp. Dr. Scrivner came in and started examining her. When I told him about the plums he said, "That's not it." He kept working with her, then he looked up at me and said, "Where's Bradley?"

"He's in the lower field."

"Go get him."

"He's plowing and he ain't going to like this. Why do I need to go get him?"

Dr. Scrivner replied, "Doris has polio. The nearest hospital that can treat her is in Birmingham and I don't think she'll live to get there. I want you to go get Bradley so I can talk to him. Then I'm going to go back to the office and make arrangements to get her moved to the hospital."

Daddy was a mile and a half down the road. I took off running all the way down to the field where he was plowing what we called the ten-acre field. It was flat enough and long enough that from one end you could barely see the tractor at the other end. Well, I met Daddy midways and told him what the doctor had said. Daddy pulled me up on the tractor with him and drove to the house where Dr. Scrivner told him he didn't think Doris would live until we got her to Birmingham, but we had to try.

The only thing I knew about polio was that it was a crippling disease. I didn't know that it was popping up in different places across the nation every summer leaving thousands of people— mainly children—dead or crippled and that scientists were rushing to find the cause and cure. I didn't know that President Franklin D. Roosevelt hadn't been able to walk on his own because of polio or that anyone in Fayette County had ever had it. My education started at that moment.

Dr. Scrivner went back to his office and called the hospital in Fayette. They sent an ambulance, two nurses and a doctor. I'd never heard an ambulance anywhere except Chicago, and we could hear this one coming through Berry. I don't ever in my lifetime remember being as scared as I was when I heard that siren. The road from Highway 18 to our house was about a mile and a half long. I stepped out on the porch and I could see the dust boiling, then the ambulance barreling toward us. I didn't know what to do. This was my child in that bed dying.

Daddy called Aunt Lois in Fayette. She and Uncle Robert had a good car and told us they would come pick us up. In the meantime we changed clothes and got partially presentable. I went next door to Gay Beard's to call and leave a message where Calvin lived. Gay got the switchboard operator at the YMCA on the phone and handed the receiver to me. I didn't even know which end to put up to my ear. When Gay realized that I had never used a telephone before, she showed me how and I left word for Calvin to meet us at the hospital.

When we finally got to see Doris, all we saw was her little head sticking out of the end of a noisy metal monster with gadgets and gauges all over it. A nurse told me that it was an iron lung, and its purpose was to force Doris to breathe by pumping air into the chamber where she laid and then sucking it out to make her lungs expand and deflate. She needed this because she had bulbar polio that affected the part of her brain that controlled breathing.

No one knew if she would live or die, and one of us needed to be with her at all times. During that time my life became enclosed in University Hospital in the big city of Birmingham. Daddy was already in the middle of planting a crop and Clara was expecting her third child, so I ended up being Doris's chief caretaker. I was a scared eighteen-year-old, the most ignorant country thing the hospital staff had ever seen. I didn't know how to talk to a doctor or ask   questions; I didn't know how to find my way around the hospital or even how to make a phone call.

At that point I almost abandoned Danny. I would take him to Calvin's mother on Sunday night, then Calvin and I would go to Birmingham—usually someone would drive us because Calvin still wasn't driving in the city. We hadn't had time to find a place to live, so Calvin would go to his room at the Y and I'd stay at the hospital until Friday night or whenever someone from home would come to relieve me. I ate out of the vending machines and washed up in a bathroom sink.

Mother had a sister, Gladys, who lived in Birmingham. After Doris and I had been there for a week or so, Gladys sent her husband to bring me to her house for some time off. I had not slept in a bed the whole time we had been at the hospital and only took little naps when I could. At Gladys's I took a shower and had not been asleep long when somebody from the hospital came to pick me up. Doris had gotten so upset when she discovered I wasn't there that they couldn't calm her down.

I went back to the hospital and stayed there for the rest of the two months she was in her iron lung. She needed me. If her nose itched, she couldn't scratch it. She couldn't feed herself or turn herself over, which was important for someone with impaired lungs. Watching over Doris was a full time job.

The nurses eventually realized that we were poor as church mice and didn't know how to do anything. They started ordering Doris a tray for lunch and supper, knowing she couldn't eat it and I could. Some of the nurses would bring me coffee and a sausage biscuit in the morning and they let me use the nurses' bathroom to bathe and change clothes. Calvin would go to work at Joslyn and every evening he would take a streetcar or a taxi down to University Hospital. We'd eat at a hole-in-the-wall across from the hospital and order things that didn't cost more than a dollar. At bedtime I either slept on the floor of Doris's room or would go down to the lobby, which closed at 9:00, and sleep on the long benches that ran along the walls. Sometimes Calvin would spend the night with me; after he started driving in Birmingham, we'd sleep in the car if it wasn't too hot. The nurses told me that they would come get me if Doris woke up and needed me. On Friday night or Saturday morning Daddy or someone from his family would come and stay with her while we went home and spent some time with Danny.

During the early part of her stay in the hospital, Doris was kept in isolation to keep her free from infection. Visitors had to have a special pass to be on the 12th floor and had to scrub up and put on hospital gowns before they could touch her.

After Doris had been in the hospital for a week or so our mother, the woman who had abandoned her when she was a baby, showed up. I was surprised because Gay Beard had told us that when Doris was taken to the hospital, she hurried over to Mother's to see if she wanted to go to Birmingham. Mother didn't stop doing her laundry; she just said, "Well, she's Bradley's little hare-brained SOB; let him watch out after her." But suddenly she was downstairs asking for permission to visit Doris in isolation. A nurse took me out in the hallway to ask if they should let her up. Doris wasn't conscious, but we didn't know how much she understood, so we were careful about what we talked about in front of her. Knowing how disagreeable Mother could be and knowing that Doris was hanging onto life by a thread, I said no. So once again Mother was turned away from one of her children in a hospital. She didn't come back even after Doris got out of isolation.

After Doris had been in the iron lung for about two months, the doctors decided that she was probably going to survive. They started physical therapy to teach her how to breathe on her own. They did that with a rocking bed. It frightened me the first time I saw Doris on it. They would strap her in upright position, with her head above her feet, on something that looked like a seesaw, then suddenly flip her upside down, heels over head. The motion of the bed was timed to make her inhale as she went down and exhale as she came up.

Once Doris could breathe again, she was transferred to the Crippled Children's Hospital across the street for rehab. She stayed there off and on for five years. Doris would never have survived any of this had it not been for the March of Dimes. Daddy wouldn't have either. When she was diagnosed with polio, the March of Dimes stepped in and paid for everything. For a good while she wore a body brace similar to an old corset that buckled up. She wore a leg brace and a built-up shoe. When she was learning to walk again she had to have arm crutches. Later she had a complete spinal fusion and stayed in a body cast about ten months. The March of Dimes assumed all of her hospital bills. They paid for all the therapies that she had over the years; they paid for all of her special shoes and braces—and as a growing child, she had to replace them often.

Once Doris was situated in rehab, Daddy fell into his old mode of walking away from his troubles. Doris was out of his sight and out of his mind. During the years of hospitalizations that followed, he expected me to assume all the responsibility and I did. But since we were not allowed to be at Crippled Children's except during visiting hours, Calvin and I finally had time to find a place to live in Birmingham and to reclaim our little boy. ❧

After Doris left the University Hospital in Birmingham, I visited her often at the Crippled Children's Hospital. I was probably 18 years old when this photo was taken.

Mt. Olive

*After we moved to Birmingham Calvin discovered beer.
He spent a lot of time at the "top of the hill" with friends
after work. This was taken in the early 1960s.*

Calvin and I drove around looking for an apartment in
Birmingham and found one in Norwood, a neighborhood that had
been elite in the early 1900s. It was directly north of downtown and
convenient to the streetcar that went by Crippled Children's
Hospital. We moved into our part of the grand old house that Mrs.
Myrtle Lutes had divided into apartments after her husband died. I
was happy to have Danny with us again, but with him I couldn't visit
Doris as often as I wanted. When Calvin worked second shift he
would stay with Danny, and sometimes he would bring Danny to the
hospital while I was visiting Doris. She would go to the window and
wave down to him. He still remembers that.

Calvin really wanted to get out of the city, though, and when a
friend at work told him that his mother-in-law in Mt. Olive was

looking for someone to live in an apartment in her house, Calvin had to see it. Soon we were following his friend to Mt. Olive. After half an hour of driving I thought "My God, where's this person taking us?"

We drove north about 20 miles on U.S. Highway 31 past beer joints, car lots, mom-and-pop grocery stores, and tourist courts and then through some open countryside before we got to the little town of Gardendale. There we turned left onto Mt. Olive Road and before long we were in the country again. Mt. Olive was just an unincorporated scattering of plain little houses, churches, and food stores with gas pumps in front. Many of the houses, as well as the big white wood-frame school building at the center, had been built in the late 1930s as part of President Roosevelt's New Deal. They originally sat on five-acre lots so that people could grow their own food, since they'd lost their jobs in the steel mills and coal mines during the Depression. By the time we got there in 1954 most of the lots had been divided up and it wasn't a farm community, but Mt. Olive was the type of place where homesick children of farmers wanted to live while they worked in the city.

So we moved to Mt. Olive into Grandma Goins's little house on Violet Drive. She kept two rooms for herself, and Calvin and I and Danny took three rooms. After I found out that I could ride into Birmingham on McClellan Bus Lines for 50 cents and get a transfer back, Mt. Olive didn't seem so far away from Doris. And it wasn't too far from our folks in Fayette County. Taking back roads we could get there in two hours.

After a year we moved in with another widow woman, Mrs. Ada Hancock, and before long I made friends with most of the older women in the neighborhood. One was Mrs. Johnson who lived across the street in a house she shared with her son Elmer and his wife Evelyn. Mrs. Johnson didn't like her daughter-in-law and would say bad things about her. I didn't know Evelyn, but she and I would throw up a hand when we saw each other coming and going. Then Evelyn quit her job as a beautician and started staying at home. I said to myself, "I'm going to find out how bad that person is." I went across the street and introduced myself. I found out she was from Louisville, Kentucky. She had met Elmer while he was in the service there and married him. I think that was the hitch with her mother-in-law. Mrs. Johnson had probably had a daughter-in-law picked out and he married somebody she didn't know. Soon Evelyn and I discovered we had a lot in common—including the same birthday and anniversary. Also she was dreadfully homesick and I was really missing my brothers and sisters. So Evelyn and I made a pretty good pair. Calvin and Elmer hit if off too, and within a three-week period we had made a fast and hard friendship that lasted many long years.

There were periods when Doris didn't need me and I had some free time. During one of those periods Evelyn and I established a routine. On Fridays we would take the bus into town and spend all day shopping. Danny was about five years old. We would drag the poor little fellow along with us and just wear him out. We'd try on clothes. You would have thought we were going to buy out the store the way we'd go into those places. We didn't have any money, but the sales clerks didn't know that. We just looked at everything and could tell you from one week to the next what was new on the shelf at Newberry's, Loveman's, and Pizitz. Sometimes we'd have enough money for lunch but that would be it. Krystal Hamburgers had just come to Birmingham and located down the street from Newberry's. We'd eat a few of those tiny burgers and think they were the best things we'd ever put in our mouths. Finally we would walk down to First Avenue North where Elmer worked at Star Provisions, a meat-packing house, and catch a ride home with him. Calvin and Elmer both got paid on Fridays. If we saw anything we just had to have, we'd get them to take us downtown on Saturday and they'd drink a beer together while we finished our shopping.

Their friendship was a Godsend to us. Elmer was raised in a rural part of Jefferson County. Calvin and I wanted to get out in the woods and Elmer knew where all the woodsy places were. And Evelyn was there to take care of Danny and the children that came later when I needed to be at the hospital with Doris.

Calvin was still working at Joslyn but decided to take a part time job working on afternoons and Saturdays at a filling station in Mt. Olive. We needed the money, but money was secondary to Calvin. He just enjoyed being out, chatting with people as he pumped gas and wiped their windshields. He loved helping people fix little problems they were having with their cars. Another thing he loved was going out to bars with his buddies. This was new to Calvin. We didn't have bars in Fayette County, and though there was a big trade in moonshine there, neither of our families had much to do with it. Calvin didn't go to bars on weekdays very often, but on most Friday and Saturday nights he wouldn't come home until 2 a.m. or so, and he'd be drunk. I talked myself into accepting that because I knew Calvin had married so young that he hadn't had time to get his wildness out and he was making up for lost time. But then I discovered that he was doing things I couldn't accept.

One Saturday Calvin came to pick Danny and me up at my daddy's after we'd spent a week helping with the farming. As we were driving back to Mt. Olive, I could sense that something was wrong and I made Calvin talk about it. He didn't want to tell me, but finally he said that he had a girl friend. That's what he called her—his girlfriend. He had met her at the filling station. She had a new '55 Chevrolet—they were the popular car of the day—and she let him drive it. He had fun with her and planned to keep on having fun with her. In an instant all my dreams of a happy family vanished. I felt physically ill. Everything was over and I could only think of divorce, the thing I had always vowed I would never do. I cried the rest of the two-hour trip home and when we got there, I grabbed some clothes for Danny and me and made Calvin drive me back to his father's house.

It was almost dark when we got there. Calvin got out of the car, set my bags on the ground and drove away. Mr. Kimbrell was over at the barn feeding the animals but stopped and came over to me.

"What's going on?"

"Calvin has another woman and we're going to have to get a divorce."

"Why didn't you tell me that when you got out of the car? I'da given him a whupping before he left here."

I stayed with the Kimbrells that night and sent word for Daddy to come get me the next day. Of course Daddy started telling me how sorry Calvin was and that I should never go back to him. Daddy's married life wasn't the greatest in the world; I don't know why he felt like he could give me advice. I guess he was trying to be fatherly. Anyway, that night he had to drive Clara to church. They wanted me to go with them but Danny and I stayed home and went to bed. I had dozed off to sleep and suddenly it seemed like someone was physically shaking me. I sat straight up in the bed and just as clearly as if He were in the room with me, I heard the Lord say, "Go home."

By the time they got back from church, I had our suitcase packed, Danny dressed, and we were sitting by the door waiting for Daddy to take us home.

Daddy said, "I'm not taking you." I got Danny by the arm, grabbed my suitcase by the other hand, and started out the door. Daddy saw that I was going to walk to Mt. Olive if he didn't drive me, so he got Karrold and they took me home. When we pulled up to the house, we saw Calvin's car. I wouldn't let Daddy get out, because I knew there would be a confrontation. I still had my key and I went in. I don't think Calvin and I spoke that night, but for many years afterward we talked and fought about that woman and the others that came along after her. And for years I debated with myself about whether or not to leave him.

I reminded myself that Calvin had just been 17 when we married and hadn't had any girlfriends before me. He'd never had a youth. I told myself that it was common for working class men to fool around on their wives. And even though his drinking and girlfriends were painful and humiliating to me, I knew that Calvin was still the right person for me. We had the same ideals. We wanted to have children and raise them right. I loved him and believed I should honor my marriage vows, even if Calvin didn't. Mostly I stayed with Calvin because I was determined to give Danny a good home, and I didn't believe I could do it by myself.

After a brief fling with the woman in the '55 Chevy, Calvin straightened out and became a family man again. Life was good—we were excited about Danny starting school, we had good friends, and we were happy to discover that I was pregnant with Kathy. We had settled into Mt. Olive so well that people back in Berry regarded us as city folks.

My biggest worry at the time was Doris. Her polio had left her with use of only one lung, so she never had a strong respiratory system and was in the hospital with pneumonia at least twice a year. Many times the doctors said she had no chance of surviving, but she would recover and go home to stay with Daddy or my grandmother until she got sick again. Then they would bring her back to Birmingham because the hospital in Fayette wasn't capable of caring for her and because she couldn't get the March of Dimes benefits there. Evelyn was happy to keep Danny while I was on short visits to Doris, but during the crisis periods when we would be at the hospital for a week or more, I didn't feel I could impose on her.

Mother or Daddy didn't help me in any of this even though they were her parents. I don't think Daddy was capable of handling the emotional trauma. Some people can't. His way of handling it was just to walk away from it. And Calvin sometimes would come home and sometimes would decide to go get a beer or do something other than come home. I couldn't leave Danny with him. So I would drive two hours to Fayette County, leave Danny with Calvin's mother and then drive back to Birmingham to stay with Doris. When Doris was about thirteen she had one of her worst bouts with pneumonia. This particular time they weren't able to get her to breathe like she should and had to do an emergency tracheotomy with Doris under only a local anesthetic. So that she wouldn't get hysterical, I had to stand and hold her hand while they cut an air hole in her neck.

Afterwards they put her in a semi-private room and gave me the bed next to her, because I was eight months pregnant and big as a barrel. While I stayed there I learned how to go into that tracheotomy and suction it without hurting her.

I couldn't count on Calvin to take care of Danny or Kathy and the other babies who came later. Like most men of the time, he saw his role as providing financial support and discipline for the children, but he wouldn't watch after them, change their diapers, or get up in the middle of the night with them. He didn't see those things as his responsibility. Caring for Doris, however, was a different matter—I knew that he would be there when she needed him. Doris could be sitting up talking to you and 15 minutes later she might be gasping for breath, deathly sick with pneumonia. That's how fragile her condition was. At times when she was too sick to walk into the doctor's office, she would stay in the car and Dr. Dunnavant would come out to see her. There was a time she had been with us for a few days because she was a little bit puny. One morning she woke up so sick that I couldn't carry her to the doctor. If I took her straight to the hospital without doctor's orders we might have to wait in the emergency room for half a day. So I called Dr. Dunnavant and asked him to come see her at our house. He came on his lunch hour, listened to her and said, "Yeah, she has pneumonia. Get her to Carraway Hospital." He picked up the phone and made arrangements to get her admitted. Doris started crying and he said, "Well, what are you crying for, honey? It's all right. You're going to be all right when you get in the hospital."

"I can't go."

"Why can't you go?"

"I can't go to the hospital until Calvin gets here and carries me."

He turned around and said, "Where in the hell is Calvin?"

"He's at work."

Dr. Dunavant called Calvin on his job and told him to get off work and take Doris to the hospital. Calvin did. He and Doris were just that way about each other, and their relationship made it hard for me to think about leaving Calvin during the bad times.

Kathy was born in November of 1957 and now we had the ideal family, a little boy six years old and a new baby girl. At this time Calvin was still going to bars on weekends, but I don't know if he had any new girlfriends. I never tried very hard to find out since there wasn't much I could do about it. Elmer and Evelyn were aware of what was going on between Calvin and me, but they didn't let it affect our friendship. If they wanted to do something on a Friday night when Calvin was out on the town, they'd come by and pick us up and we'd go do whatever it was.

"Is Calvin up at the top of the hill?" That's what we called a string of beer joints between Mt. Olive and Birmingham. "Come on," they'd say, "We'll be back before he gets home." But sometimes Calvin would join us and we'd have a better time.

Elmer had a passion for cars. His car was his pride and whatever else happened on a weekend, it got washed and shined from one end to the other. He had bought a brand new Pontiac hardtop, a pretty thing, about the time that Kathy was born. Evelyn invited us to go with them in it to Louisville and spend Labor Day weekend with her parents. She and I had everything packed when Calvin and Elmer got in from work. I had bathed Danny and had his pajamas on him, ready to put him to bed on a quilt on the floorboard. We made a little bed for Kathy on the back seat between me and Evelyn—this was before infant carriers and seat belts—and we put all our suitcases in the trunk. When we got into Tennessee, we started getting cold and Elmer rolled the windows up. We got on a little further in northern Tennessee and we got colder. We stopped at a filling station and got all of our sweaters out of our suitcases and put them on. We were still cold and the further north we went, the colder we got. It took about eight or nine hours to drive into Louisville and by the time we got there at 4 o'clock the next morning, we were icebergs. Danny and Kathy, wrapped in quilts, were the only two warm people in that car.

Elmer said he wasn't going to wake Evelyn's mother up so early.

"We're going to go somewhere and get us a cup of coffee and warm up." While we were drinking our hot chocolate and coffee one of us happened to ask, "Elmer, does that car have a heater?" Four supposed-to-be adults had driven all that way in a brand new car and until that moment no one had thought about turning on the heater. That was a lifetime joke. Every time Elmer traded cars we'd ask, "Have you got a heater?"

We remained close to Elmer and Evelyn for many years but our shopping trips together ended in the early '60s when protests against segregation began and we didn't think it was wise to go downtown. Though we were only about 20 miles from Birmingham, all we knew of the children's marches, water hoses and police dogs were what we saw on television along with the rest of the world. None of us had ever heard of Bull Connor before but now we were embarrassed by him and hated the way he made folks in Birmingham look like devils. We grieved for the four little girls killed at the 16th Street Baptist Church and prayed for their families. But mainly we plowed on with our lives in Mt. Olive, raising Danny, Kathy and the two little girls who came soon after, Nina and Cindy.

With four children, it was time to get a place of our own. We had been eyeing a little house on Swann Road, a winding road with houses of all sizes, shapes, dollar values, and uses. For instance, the house across the street from us had a body shop in the back yard. The one we wanted looked like a little box with asbestos siding and a small concrete front porch. When we got to go inside, the children saw bare hardwood floors. They ripped their shoes off and wildly slid around the living room in sock feet. They were thrilled when we bought it but Cindy was disappointed we filled it with furniture and it wasn't a skating rink anymore. It was just a plain little three-bedroom house, probably 40 years old. It needed fixing up, which we knew Calvin could do. The best thing about it was that we could afford it. The next best thing about it was the roomy kitchen with lots of cabinets and counters and space for a big table at one end. The living room was large and the bedrooms were tiny. We rationed them out: one for Calvin and I; one for Kathy, Nina, and Cindy; and one for Danny. We all shared the little bathroom.

Our surprise baby, Scott, came at a bad time. Calvin had gone back to drinking and was having an affair. I was fed up and leaning more toward divorce than I ever had. My oldest child was 18, my youngest was 6, and now my fifth child was on its way. This was the only accident I'd had—we'd planned our other children and knew exactly when they were conceived. I had no idea when I got pregnant and I wasn't the least bit happy about it because we didn't have any money and I didn't know if my marriage was going to last. I was sick the whole nine months, from the time I got up in the morning until I went to bed at night.

The only nice thing about the pregnancy was my intuition that this child was a boy. When Danny was three or four, he'd had the mumps and given them to Calvin and me. The doctor told Calvin that from now on all our children would be the same sex. After we had three girls in a row we were starting to believe him. Calvin wondered what in the world he would do with four girls, but we couldn't help feeling that the child I was carrying was male. "If you have a son, I'll buy you a dozen roses," he promised.

I went to the hospital on Sunday night and was in labor through the night and into the next day. Evelyn stayed with the children and sent them on to school as usual on Monday morning. After the baby finally came I remember Calvin waking me up to say he was leaving to get my roses in honor of Scotty Jackson Kimbrell.

The only one who wasn't happy about having a new brother was Cindy, who had been Calvin's little buddy for six years. She went hunting with him and considered herself Daddy's favorite, but suddenly there was not enough room in Calvin's lap for her when he held Scotty. She'd cry and ask, "Can we take him back?" But to Nina he was a real live breathing baby doll, and she liked nothing better than to sit and rock him.

I was now 33 and living the life that I had dreamed of when I was ten years old. I had a husband I loved, five good children and a house that didn't belong to someone else. I hadn't counted on Doris getting polio or Calvin drinking and being unfaithful, but I wasn't about to abandon my dreams.

Calvin had long stretches on the wagon before he would fall off again. A lot of it depended on who he was working with. If his work buddies said "When we get off at 3:30, let's stop in for a beer," he'd do it. With the bars came the women. Calvin was now middle-aged and had lost most of his hair. What remained was prematurely gray, but he was still handsome. And his personality carried more weight than his looks. He listened to people and talked to them about their lives, and that attracted women to him. Men are easily tempted. You can take a woman who doesn't have much going for her—if she sets out to get a man's attention, she'll usually find a way.

Calvin gave into that temptation more than once and he fully expected me to two-time him like he did me. He anticipated my revenge and I couldn't convince him that adultery was the furthest thing from my mind. I was taking care of Doris and the five kids and getting them to school and doctors and sports, pretty much on my own. If I wanted to play around with another man, when would I do it?

Scott was born in 1969 about six weeks before Danny graduated from high school. Clockwise in this photo are baby Scott, me, Danny, Kathy, Nina and Cindy.

Fun-Daddy

Calvin enjoyed Halloween with his children. Standing behind Calvin in this 1972 snapshot are Cindy, Kathy, and Nina. Scott is sitting on his lap.

Calvin was a good father even when he wasn't a good husband. He didn't miss a football game as long as Danny and Scott were playing and was involved in all the girls' softball games. He supported me in making them do their homework and go to church. He worried about his children, and if one were sick he would call me from each job site and let me know how to reach him. A neighbor was here one day when he called and she said, "My husband is a deacon in the church and he does not do for his family like Calvin Kimbrell does." And she'll tell you that now. She says, "He cared more for his children and what his family was and wanted to be than half the people in church did."

Most of the time the children loved to be around him. At the big Kimbrell family gatherings he'd play the guitar and sing. It tickled the kids when he'd put their names into songs like "Coming Round the Mountain." After work he'd sit on the porch, drink a cold beer, and watch them play kickball in the yard. The next thing you know he'd be down there playing with them.

On Sundays when we weren't fishing he would drive them to the gravel pit. It was an area where the county stored gravel for road repairs, but folks around Mt. Olive considered it a playground and took their children there to slide down the gravel piles and dig in them. Other times he would load the kids in the back of his truck and haul them all afternoon over every Podunk back country road in Blount and Walker counties. He started all of them driving when they were about 12. Learning to drive was a family thing. During a Sunday drive he would pull over and say something like "I've got to get out a minute. Let Sis up here in the driver's seat." Kathy says she still can remember that sudden excitement and nervousness that came over her when it was her turn.

He usually supported my household rules, but when he was being "Fun-Daddy," as Cindy called him on his good days, he bent them in the children's favor. One of my big rules was that we all eat our meals together at the table. A children's movie, *Willie Wonka and the Chocolate Factory*, had been advertised constantly on TV and they were excited about watching it Sunday evening. That night, though, Calvin didn't show up for dinner when he said he would. I had fixed a big supper and told them we had to wait on him to eat it. That's not what they wanted to hear.

"Mama, we're going to miss it. We've waited all week to watch it."

When Calvin finally came in just as the movie was starting I said, "Dinner's on the table. Come eat it while it's hot and when we've finished and y'all have cleaned the kitchen then you can watch what's left."

Calvin, probably feeling guilty about causing dinner to be late, said, "If my kids want to watch this show, they are going to watch it." And he got them to help him move all the living room furniture back and walk the kitchen table to a place in front of the TV. It was the first, and maybe only, time they ever watched TV during dinner while they lived with me.

There were two days a year that we could count on him to be Fun-Daddy—Christmas and Halloween. Calvin loved Christmas. Even though it came at a time of year when he tended to be out of work, he insisted that we make gift baskets for our neighbors. He'd go to the farmer's market and get a case of oranges and other fruit. I'd put a jar of homemade jelly in each basket, Nina would tie a pretty bow on it, and he and the kids would deliver them house-by-house. On Christmas day he'd make sure that any elderly folks in the neighborhood who didn't have kin close by got a plate of our Christmas dinner. He also put himself in charge of getting the Christmas tree. Early in December he would start looking for one while he hunted deer. He'd come home and say, "I've got our Christmas tree picked out." Everyone would groan, knowing it would be a Charlie Brown Christmas tree, where you put on one ornament and the whole tree topples over. The branches of those little cedars would be so limber they couldn't hold a string of lights. Nina, who really cared about decorations, says he somehow managed to find the ugliest tree on the planet every year. One year we bought one off a lot and thereafter the kids would beg him for a store-bought tree.

"Nope, I've got a really gorgeous one picked out this year."

He would bring it home the day school got out for the holidays and the kids would tie the lights on and decorate it as best they could, putting near the top the three ornaments that Calvin and I have had since Danny was a baby.

On Christmas Eve the children would put their favorite pair of shoes under the tree. I'm not sure why we used shoes instead of stockings; it's just the way the Kimbrells had always done it. The kids would wake up to find shoes full of peppermint sticks, fruit, nuts, and little toys or jewelry. But they couldn't get out of bed until Santa said "Ho Ho Ho" in a big deep voice. They would lie there in agony waiting for their father, who usually had been at the top of the hill until 2 a.m., to drag himself out of bed, drink some coffee, and say "Ho Ho Ho" very dramatically. Kathy remembers the Christmas she was 17. It must have been a better than usual year for us because she got a stereo system with a turntable, a radio, an 8-track player, and two speakers. Calvin opened the front windows, put the speakers in them and blasted Christmas music out to the neighbors.

Calvin loved Halloween as much as he did Christmas. I, on the other hand, dreaded it. I didn't boycott it but I didn't get in the spirit of it the way Calvin did. The kids had to go to their closets and figure out their own costumes. They could be princesses, gypsies, pirates, or football players, but I didn't let them be witches, ghosts, goblins, or any other kind of evil thing. They would trick or treat in the neighborhood and I'd give out homemade popcorn balls to the kids who came to our house. About dusk Calvin would come home with a scary-old-man mask and say, "Y'all get in the car and we'll go by Dink's house to trick or treat." It could be Dink or Elmer or any of his beer-drinking buddies. I'd tell him he couldn't take them out because he'd been drinking and he'd say, "Well, you drive."

The children would be clamoring to go and letting me know I was being a sour puss, so I would give in. After I drove a while Calvin would say, "Now Bett, we're going to pull in here. You turn off the lights and shut the engine off and just coast into his driveway." I would do it, hating every second of the experience, while they were thinking "Mother just needs to lighten up. Daddy's in a good mood. He's playing with us." He would sneak out of the car, barely closing the door, hide in the bushes, put on his horrible mask, and then motion for the children to go to the door.

Usually his friend's wife would come to the door and say something like "It's Calvin and Bettye's kids. Aren't y'all cute? Let me go get some candy for you." Calvin would wait 'til she came back with a big bowl of candy then roar out of the bushes. The candy would fly everywhere.

"My gosh, Calvin, you nearly caused me to have a heart attack." I would sit in the car shaking my head.

My worst Halloween experience happened when Scott was about four and the others ranged up from there. Kathy was 15 or 16 and Danny was in the Army. Calvin had run out of places to take them and it was still early.

"I tell you what, run by the top of the hill."

"You are not taking my children into a bar."

"By God, they are my kids too. I said go by the top of the hill."

I started crying. "Calvin, I'm begging you. Please don't take my children into a bar."

The children were all excited. "We're going to get to go to the top of the hill! We never get to go to the top of the hill."

I could have strangled him. I stayed in the car, worried and upset, until they came out beaming and telling me what had happened. They said the men treated Calvin like he was a celebrity.

"Why, Calvin, who do you got here?"

"This one's Kathy and this one's Nina and this one's Cindy and here's my little man, Scotty."

The children, dressed like clowns and hillbillies and whoever else they found in the closet, all stood with their trick-or-treat bags held out. Of course, no one had candy to give them. After an awkward minute or two, one of them put a dollar in each bag. And the next guy thought that was a good idea and did the same. When they got back in the car the kids started digging through their bags, counting their money and saying, "This is the best Halloween ever." They each came home with about $15. I made them tithe their proceeds the next Sunday and promise not to tell anyone where they got the money. ❧

Hard Drinker

Calvin liked his beer. Sometimes he would drink a case of it a day. It didn't do any good to fuss at him; that would just make him drink more. He was the only one of the Kimbrell boys who would drink in front of his mother. When he went home, he would bring beer and put it in her refrigerator. She vowed up one side and down the other that he wasn't going to do it, but he did. One day she got a butcher knife, took his beer out behind the smoke house and started punching holes in the cans. Her aim went bad and she laid her hand open with the knife. After that Calvin kept his beer in a cooler in the car instead of her refrigerator.

Beer wasn't much of a problem, other than the fact he spent money on it that we needed for food and clothes. He could drink two cases of beer and be a jolly good fellow. He could take a teaspoon of whiskey and turn bulletproof and mean. If someone gave him a bottle of whiskey or a jar of moonshine, he couldn't stop drinking until the bottle was empty or he passed out, whichever came first. With the liquor came the women. I think Danny was the only child who knew about the women and he didn't talk about it. The others didn't need to know and I kept it from them until they were grown. It hurts to tell some of the things Calvin did off and on during 40 long years of our marriage, but I will because I know there is a happy ending.

His drinking bothered all of the children. Our sons were exposed to his bad side more than the girls because they went hunting with him in Fayette County where he, his brothers, and my brothers would drink together, brawl, almost kill each other with knives and guns, then end up crying and hugging each other. Danny, and Scott years later, were the ones he woke up in the middle of the night saying "Come get me, I'm too drunk to drive home," even though they were not old enough to have drivers' licenses. They both resented being used that way. I hated it, too, but didn't want to leave the girls alone to go get him; I just prayed until they all got home.

Nina and Kathy literally ran to their rooms and cowered when Calvin stumbled into the house loud and drunk, but Cindy, who would argue with the devil, tended to stand her ground. Her little feist dog, Mimi, was our canary in the coal mine. Calvin would have as many as 15 hunting dogs in the back yard, but only Mimi lived inside because Cindy had asthma and we had heard that a small housedog could help prevent asthma attacks. Mimi was a wonderful family dog who loved a house full of kids running around. She was devoted to sober Calvin, but feared the drunk Calvin who might stumble on her or kick at her and yell, "Get out from under my feet." Calvin drove a truck with racks of ladders that rattled as he came down the hill to our house. When we heard him coming we'd turn to Mimi who would be concentrating on the front door with her ears up straight. If she sat down and wagged her tail, we could relax and give Calvin a friendly greeting when he came in. But if she crawled into the wicker bed beside Calvin's recliner and burrowed under the cover, the kids knew to turn the TV off, pick up their shoes, run to their rooms, and start doing their homework.

Scott says that after Calvin got sober, the bad times were just water under the bridge—but he still remembers them, such as one of the hunting trips he took with his dad when he was 14. He and Calvin arrived at their hunting spot and mapped out a plan. Scott was to go to the left, Calvin would go right, they would circle around to a certain point in a couple of hours and walk back to the truck together. But Calvin didn't leave the truck; he stayed in it consuming a whole bottle of whiskey. When Scott got back, Calvin was beyond three sheets to the wind. Scott managed to push and pull him into the passenger seat and drive him home, his head banging against the window the whole way.

As they pulled into our driveway, Scott said, "Daddy, go on in and I'll get all the gear out of the truck." But Calvin said, "I'll get my gun. You get the other stuff," which is not what Scott wanted to hear. Calvin staggered in and stood teetering in front of me while he fumbled with his shotgun, trying to take the shells out before he put it away. They dropped to the floor, and as he stooped to pick them up he slowly rolled over on top of them. Scott pulled the shotgun out from under him, locked it in the cabinet, picked up the shells, and asked what we should do with Calvin. "Leave him laying," I answered. I wasn't about to move him. If he passed out on the floor, that's where he woke up. I knew he would get up the next morning and regret the whole thing.

Even when I was thoroughly upset with Calvin, I tried to stay low key around the children. The four youngest remember the Sunday morning that we were rushing around getting ready for church. It was a chaotic time—getting them fed and helping them hunt for shoes, hair bows, and Bibles at the same time. Calvin had not come home from his Saturday night drinking and I was trying to keep that off my mind by sticking to the routine. The phone rang and I recognized the voice of my next-door neighbor, Mrs. Spiegel, on the other end.

"Mrs. Kimmell," she said. She never could say "Kimbrell." "I believe Mr. Kimmell is dead."

"What?"

"Well, he's laying out there face down on your front steps."

I looked out the window and saw Calvin passed out cold on our concrete porch.

"He's not dead. He's just drunk and stupid. But thank you for calling."

It was the middle of winter. We all put on our coats and headed out the door and as the children passed by Calvin sprawled out on the steps, I said, "Don't step on your Daddy." Cindy, who was eight or nine, remembers carefully stepping around him.

When we got home from church Calvin was sitting in his recliner with a quilt wrapped around him and a cup of coffee shaking in his hand. He was shivering from lying out on the steps most of the night in freezing weather. He looked at me reproachfully and said, "The least you could have done is throw a blanket over me." I answered,

"If you are going to be dumb, you've got to be tough." Then I cooked Sunday dinner like I always did.

But there were times I couldn't conceal my sadness, such as the Christmas when one of Calvin's buddies gave him a bottle of whiskey. He had been drinking hard, but I was relieved to see that he was close to the bottom of the bottle and we were almost through with his binge. I was in the kitchen making pies when he came in with a full quart of moonshine and put it in the cabinet above the refrigerator. My spirits plunged. Thinking of the hard couple of days that would come from that jar full of whiskey, I rolled out the piecrust with tears in my eyes. Suddenly there was an explosion overhead in the cabinet and liquid began to seep out and drip on the refrigerator. Calvin accused me of destroying it, but I knew it was an act of God and silently thanked Him for it.

When Calvin was on an extended drunk, he wore on all of us. Each of the children, one by one, came to me and begged me to leave him. Nina, who had a part-time job while she was a senior in high school, told me she would get a second job and support Cindy, Scott, and me if I would divorce him. I explained that Daddy and Mother had divorced and created such chaos in our lives that I promised myself I would never do that to my children. I took my marriage vows very seriously. Those vows say "until death do us part," not "until he does something contrary to my thinking." I know people my age who have been married three or four times and they are not a bit happier the third or fourth time than they were the first time. Why go through it?

Cindy said things like "Are you crazy? Why do you stay with him?" I would answer, "Because he's your father and he's a good man and he loves y'all and he loves me. You didn't know him when he was a Christian. I did. The devil's dealing with your daddy right now but that good man is still in there." I never stopped believing that he would come back. ❧

Housekeeping

Every year I made Easter dresses for my girls, Evelyn and Elmer's daughter Deanna, and myself. Calvin joined us in our snapshots but not in churchgoing. (Back row: Elmer and Evelyn Johnson, Calvin and I. Front row: Kathy, Deanna, Nina, and Cindy.) Danny, wearing the white sports coat I made him, is in the photo on the right.

So we carried on, having good times and miserable times together. After we moved to Mount Olive in 1954, Calvin left the Joslyn plant and became a house painter. The painter's union offered an apprenticeship program that taught him to mix his own colors and prepare surfaces for painting. He did a three-year apprenticeship under a senior painter and his union named him "Apprentice of the Year" after the first year. Calvin was meticulous. When he went on a job he made sure that every nail hole and every crack was filled. If something needed to be scraped and primed, Calvin did it. He used the highest quality paints. Danny says that Calvin would put good paint on an outhouse. He mainly worked for rich folks who lived "over the mountain" south of Birmingham, and most of his customers were completely loyal to him. The pay for a union painter was pretty good, but he was out of work so much during winter and spring rains that it took all summertime to catch up. It balanced out to a get-by salary. We never knew what payday would bring and lived off money from loan companies when we came up short.

Sometimes we couldn't buy many groceries, but because of the way Calvin and I were raised, we knew how to get food. Every summer I canned and froze vegetables. My first freezer was an old International freezer that Uncle Edward had bought before we ever left Mama and Papa's. I think it was one of the first home freezers made, or at least the first I'd seen, and it weighed a ton. He kept it for a few years and then he moved to Mobile and let my daddy have it. When it got low on Freon, Daddy stopped using it. I wanted it, so Calvin swapped Daddy a gun for that freezer. A friend who worked on refrigerators put some Freon in it for me and I used that thing for 15 or 20 years. Our stove and refrigerator came by way of the second-hand store. We were lucky that we knew people who did repair work for a living and would trade their work for something we could do for them.

We had that kind of relationship with Betty and Athel Dobbs, our across-the-street neighbors. Athel ran a body shop in his back yard and helped with any car problems Calvin couldn't fix himself. Betty was always ready to babysit for my children, as I was for her three. We swapped out so much that my children called her MomBetty and hers called me MomBettye.

My next-door neighbor was buying vegetables from a couple in Corner who truck farmed. They were a Godsend for us. They would pick the first crop and take it to the farmer's market in Birmingham to get the best price for it. Then they would call me and say, "Bettye, we're going to have five bushels of peas tomorrow. Do you want them?" If I had the money I'd go get them. If I didn't have it, he would tell me to come get them anyway and pay him Saturday. If they had too much come in at a time, he'd say, "Can you come and pick ten rows of peas I've got here and pay me a little bit for them?"

I'd take my kids and we'd pick vegetables, especially tomatoes. I would buy three five-gallon buckets of them for a dollar and put them up in half-gallon jars. Nina complained that the Kimbrell kids were home canning every summer while their friends were at the beach and at camp. But all of the family loved the big pots of chili I made with some pinto beans, a bit of ground beef, and a big jar of the tomatoes we had canned.

Sometimes I'd buy ice cream and save the 5-quart containers it came in. After supper if there was something leftover, but not enough for another meal, we'd throw it in an ice-cream bucket. There might be a cup of peas or beans or a piece of chicken or a dab of macaroni and cheese. I'd stick it in the freezer and when that ice cream bucket got full I'd take it out about mid-day and let it thaw. That afternoon I'd open up some tomatoes and cook the conglomeration in a big pot. That and some cornbread or crackers were Friday night's supper and Saturday's lunch. It never tasted the same, but it was always good. Usually on Saturday night or Sunday we had a big dinner with meat and then the rest of the time it was combination dishes, like chili or spaghetti. And I would put up enough fruits that I could make pies and cakes from scratch at a very low cost.

Because Calvin didn't get much work in the winter, he had time to hunt and kept us supplied with rabbit and squirrel meat, and of course we always had fish in the freezer from our Sunday outings. The girls wouldn't eat any meat that didn't come in plastic wrap with a store label on it, but the rest of us enjoyed what Calvin brought home. He also got into beekeeping, which he learned from his father. He taught Scott how to find beehives in the woods and bring them home. We ended up with more than 25 hives in our backyard and at some of our neighbor's houses. Calvin and Scott would rob the hives on the 4th of July and turn my kitchen into the family honey factory. We extracted gallons of honey, kept what we wanted and sold the rest for $5 a quart.

Store-bought clothes were pretty much out of the question, so I learned to make ones that looked store-bought. Mama had never taught me to use a sewing machine because she was fanatical about hers and wouldn't let anyone else touch it. I bought a used sewing machine someplace, a treadle machine that had been converted to electric, and I started buying patterns. I can't tell you how frustrating it was to try to understand the directions and pick out the right fabrics for each garment. But I learned to do that and to alter clothes. If Kathy outgrew one of her church dresses, I could make one of the other girls a new dress out of it.

Easter Sunday was always a big fashion event when my girls were growing up. All across the South just about every lady and her daughters felt they had to have brand new dresses, with complementary hats, gloves, shoes, and purses for the Easter service. That involved a lot of shopping but at least I could sew the dresses myself. Every year I'd make matching ones for my three girls and Deanna, Elmer and Evelyn's girl. One year the dresses had puffy sleeves that Cindy swore she would not be caught dead in. I won the Sunday morning battle and she put it on, but during the sermon she gnawed a hole in one of the sleeves, thinking we would have to throw it away. Of course I mended it and laid it out the next Sunday with a switch beside it. She wore it with a frown and counted the months until she outgrew it.

Cindy liked some of the things I made, though. One night she had a sleepover with a friend who possessed a set of panties with the days of the week embroidered on them. Cindy came home saying that her friend must be rich to have such underwear. I made her seven pairs of panties and machine-embroidered "Sunday" through "Saturday" on them. I also made cheerleader outfits for the girls to wear to games of the Pee Wee League football team that Danny coached, and with the leftover scraps of fabric I made shoeboxes full of fancy Barbie doll clothes—faux-fur jackets, bell-bottom pants, lace wedding dresses with long trains—to give the girls for Christmas. Eventually I made wedding dresses and going-away outfits for each of them.

I sewed for the boys, too. When Danny was in high school, the stylish shirts had loops above the pleat on the back. Kids called them "fruit loops" and made a game out of sneaking up behind their friends and trying to yank the loops off. So that Danny's shirts would seem store bought I always put loops on them and I don't think any of mine ever tore off. I made the double-breasted green blazer Danny needed for choir, I made clothes for Calvin and myself, and I sewed for other people, usually in exchange for material. They'd say, "Will you make me a dress?" and I would if they agreed to buy fabric for whatever I wanted to make next.

From Mama and Papa I learned how to get by on very little money, but still it took some maneuvering to buy what the children needed on Calvin's income. I wanted all my girls to have piano lessons but couldn't afford them, so I worked out a trade with Mrs. Russell, an elderly piano teacher in the neighborhood. My girls would clean her house once a week in exchange for lessons. Cindy, who just wanted to be outside playing ball, called that a double whammy, having to clean a grumpy old lady's house to pay for something she despised. None of them learned to play, but at least the opportunity was there and they could have latched on to it if they had music in them.

I made sure my kids had money for school supplies, lunches, and school pictures. If their teachers were collecting PTA dues or fees for field trips, somehow I found a way to send that money. When Scott was a senior in high school it seemed very important for him to have a football jacket. That jacket—which hasn't been off a hanger for 25 years—cost nearly $300. We were talking about it years later and I confessed that I couldn't buy groceries for three weeks after we bought it. Scott said, "I know, Mama, but you fed us anyway."

And somehow, in the midst of all my cooking and cleaning and sewing, I started quilting again. We had gas space heaters that kept us warm at night without piles of quilts but I guess those bags of scraps left over from making my children's clothes called to me. I needed to turn them into something. Quilting didn't seem so bad without a stern grandmother hovering over me demanding I rip out the crooked stitches. And after a trip to the State Fair in Birmingham in 1970, my attitude toward quilting changed from mild interest to enthusiasm. I walked through an exhibition hall filled with flower arrangements, canned goods, cakes and pies, crocheted pieces, and a good number of quilts. The quilts were nothing out of the ordinary. Mainly they were based on old-fashioned patterns like the Double Wedding Ring, Dutch Boy and Girl, and Grandmother's Flower Garden, but they were a step above the utilitarian strip quilts my grandmother made and they fascinated me.

I had learned to do a double wedding ring quilt from Mama, but didn't have the pattern anymore. I managed to get one some place and then gathered up all the sewing scraps I had in the house. I don't think I bought anything except the backing and the stuffing for that quilt. I made what I considered to be a fairly decent patchwork quilt from scraps of the children's clothes and found out how to enter it in the fair. That year we went to the craft exhibition right away to find out how my quilt did. Lo and behold, there was a blue ribbon on it. Well, did that ever blow my cap off. I'd never won any sort of prize in my life and I sure liked the feeling. The fact that someone thought my work was good enough to win a prize motivated me, and I started buying quilting magazines and looking for ideas. I found a picture of a patchwork quilt called the Missouri Daisy. I was still using my sewing scraps rather than buying cloth in coordinating colors, so patchwork patterns appealed to me. I followed the guidelines in the magazine pretty closely and the only thing I did different was use dark thread instead of white to quilt it with. That year my Missouri Daisy quilt got Best of Show and from then on I was hooked. For the next 20 years I entered a quilt in the fair and the children loved running into the exhibition hall before I got there so they could be the first to report if I had a big blue ribbon.

I was addicted—not to making quilts to keep my family warm, but to the process of creating art in my own way. Over the years I began to teach myself every sort of quilting technique I could find and when I mastered it, I'd do variations to make it my own. I wanted people to know a quilt was mine without reading the label. ❧

Danny

This is Danny in his senior year at Mortimer Jordan High School in 1969.

If life consisted of just feeding, clothing, housing, educating, entertaining, and comforting your family, there would be plenty enough to occupy your every thought and make you fall into bed exhausted every night. But those are only the things you keep doing while the huge, hulking affairs of life grab you and demand all your energy and strength. There was a period of ten years in which the big things—war, death, and cancer—hit us one after the other while I, with a husband I couldn't count on, was just trying to get our children raised.

My little companion since I was 14 years old, was about to leave home. In high school he was a tall gangly football player who made good grades in the subjects he enjoyed and barely passed those he didn't. His sisters idolized him and thought he was the handsomest and smartest boy alive. He was the only one who could get Cindy out of bed in the morning. He'd say, "If you get up, I'll give you a piggy back ride," and bring her to breakfast on his shoulders, warning her when to duck her head under the doorframes.

Danny was the only boy at Mortimer Jordan High School who took typing because I insisted that all my children know how to type. His senior yearbook has a picture of the typing class with only one member not wearing a pretty little dress. The caption identified him as Danny "Sue" Kimbrell. That didn't stop him from taking more business courses, though, and joining FBLA, the Future Business Leaders of America. When he graduated in May 1969, a few months after Scott was born, he had been named Mr. FBLA of Alabama and had just returned from the national convention in Dallas where he had won third place in typing and calculator skills.

He wasn't interested in academics, but the war in Vietnam was on everyone's mind and Danny knew he should go to college to be exempt from the draft. The military had established a lottery system to determine the order that it would call young men to serve. Danny got a low number, 46, and was classified 1A, meaning that he was near the top of the draft list and fit for service. The only way he could avoid going to Vietnam was to get an education deferment, but we were as poor as we'd ever been and couldn't help with tuition. Calvin made enough to pay the utilities, groceries, and payment on our little house and that was all.

Danny registered at Jefferson State, a two-year community college nearby, and took business courses that he paid for by working in the college's jobs placement office during the day and running the switchboard at night. To make better pay he joined the carpenter's union in Birmingham, became an apprentice carpenter, and helped build a shopping mall in Tuscaloosa, an hour away. He would get up at 4:30 a.m., drive to Bessemer, ride with six men in a truck to Tuscaloosa, and work all day. He would get home in time to drive to class, fall into bed at 11:00 p.m. and then get up and start over again. Something had to go, and Danny decided it would be college.

I knew what it was as soon as I saw it in the mailbox. Calvin was home for lunch and Milford's wife was visiting. I was warming up a pot of chili when I saw the mail truck stop, and I decided to check the mail before Calvin went back to work. After I pulled the draft notice out of the box I came in, sat down at the table, and cried. I usually can keep my emotions under control, but this time I couldn't talk enough to tell anyone what I was crying about. Finally Calvin read it and understood.

Recruiters from all branches of the military had been courting Danny for months. When he got his notice he called the Army recruiter because he wanted to fly helicopters. I was relieved when it turned out that he couldn't do that because he was colorblind. He asked what other specialties were available and the recruiter read him a list. Danny stopped him when he got to "clerk" and said, "That I can do."

He reported for duty on Easter Sunday, 1971, and there were no new dresses, hats, and gloves or fishing trips that day. He went to Fort Campbell in Kentucky for basic training and was the top graduate in his company, which entitled him to take a two-week leadership course before he went to Fort Knox for his advanced individual training. He took every kind of training he could get to delay going to Vietnam, but eventually he got sent there, near the end of the war.

I can't tell you what it was like having a son there. Only a wife or mother of a Vietnam veteran can understand. It's like losing someone. You shy away from cooking the dishes you know he likes; you don't want to hear the music he listened to or go to the games he played. You sit straight up in the middle of the night and wonder "Am I awake because he's been killed?" I felt this way even though I thought he was a clerk working in a safe office far from the front lines. It was many years later that I learned that his unit had no infantry support and did their own guard duties and patrols. He drove an armored personnel carrier, threw grenades during firefights, and did body counts after they were over.

And, of course, there were the war protesters on the news every night and the draft dodgers going to Canada. I resented those people. Here I was, dirt poor, unable to pay tuition and my child ends up in Vietnam. We didn't want him to go, but once he was called, we knew he had to go and defend his country. We believed what our leaders told us: Communism will spread throughout Southeast Asia and eventually the world if we don't stop the Communists from taking over South Vietnam. Calvin and I were patriotic; we were brought up that way. So off Danny went and the protesters made him feel like a criminal. Stories were circulating about returning vets being called "baby killers" and being spat upon as they returned from duty. During a layover at Love Field in Dallas on his way home, Danny changed into jeans and a tee shirt and felt bad about taking off a uniform he was proud of. The whole Vietnam experience was gut-wrenching for our family.

Vietnam was not the only cause of turmoil for me at the time. Before he was drafted Danny had started dating a girl named Theresa who was still in high school, and he kept in touch with her while he went through his military training. Danny says that he mentioned that they might get married someday, and before he knew it, the wedding planners were at the door. He was 20 and needed to be 21 to marry without our permission. Her parents started coming to our house every day trying to convince Calvin and me to sign for Danny to get married and I refused to do it. "Theresa needs to be in school. She doesn't need to be off in some Army camp," I told them, and they promised that they would keep her at home with them and in school while Danny was in the service. That pacified Calvin. He went to the courthouse with them and signed.

We were betrayed. On the day before the wedding Danny revealed that Theresa was going back with him to Fort Benjamin Harrison in Indiana. Her parents sent him money to rent her an apartment; gave them a car to drive to Indiana, and packed up everything she would need. It was too late to do anything about it, except shanghai Danny and send him back to Indiana without her. Don't think that didn't occur to us. But we didn't, and the wedding went forward with our family not speaking to Theresa's. We went to the ceremony and came straight home. Through the whole process of Theresa's parents begging our consent, lying to us about their intentions, and putting on the wedding, I felt like something precious was being stolen from me and I could do nothing to stop it. Resistance was as futile as being mad at a disease that is taking away a loved one. I couldn't tolerate being around Theresa and her parents, so all I could do was stay away.

When Danny left for Vietnam in 1972 Theresa was three months pregnant. When he returned a year later, Theresa and baby Laura joined him at Fort McPherson outside of Atlanta. They lived together in an apartment but with his post-traumatic stress—undiagnosed at the time—and her immaturity, the marriage was doomed. After a big blowout, she called her family for help and when they showed up Danny kept them away with an old shotgun that he'd gotten from Calvin. The next day after work he returned to an empty apartment. She had left him and taken the baby, the furniture, the money he had saved up in Vietnam, and everything else of value. He didn't hire a lawyer to get it back. He did try to stay in contact with the baby, but without Theresa's cooperation, that didn't work. Only after Laura was grown and on her own was he able to visit her.

The Danny who came home from Vietnam was different from the one who left Mt. Olive. His future didn't seem as bright as it had when he was in high school. After his divorce from Theresa became final, he married Denise, who he met in Atlanta, and together they raised five children. Like mine, his children have done well even though Danny and Denise endured the same kinds of hardships that Calvin and I did, hardships I had prayed none of my children would ever have to face. ❧

Doris

Doris did not let polio stop her from graduating with her class from Berry High School in 1963. This is her senior picture.

While our thoughts were in Vietnam, my grandparents were reaching the ends of their lives back in Fayette County. Mama had a stroke and was only ill for a few weeks before she died. Papa lived for another year and a day, the whole time feeling confused and discontented. He lost interest in everything. Even though they had fought like demons throughout their marriage, everyone said that Papa just grieved himself to death when she was gone. Mama and Papa had plenty of children and grandchildren left in Fayette County to nurse them through their old age, so I didn't do that. I was needed here to take care of my five plus Doris.

She was now close to 30, tall, and extremely fragile. She wore a complete leg brace on her right leg and a built-up shoe. There was a visible curvature to her spine that made her left shoulder two inches higher than her right. Doris had a pretty face, fixed her hair stylishly, and wore attractive clothes that I tailored to fit her.

Despite her illness, or perhaps because of it, she graduated from high school—the only one of her brothers and sisters who did. The Birmingham Public School system had a staff of teachers who served young patients at the Crippled Children's Clinic, and Doris completed four grades while she was there. Whenever she was well, she would return to Berry and attend public school. Regardless of the disruptions caused by her polio, she managed to graduate with her class at Berry High School. When she walked onto the ball field to get her diploma, the audience, faculty, and graduates all stood and clapped. They had been rooting for her since she was nine.

Doris went to business college in Birmingham and got an office job at the State Crippled Children's Service there. Before long she was serving on advisory panels concerning the design of restrooms, ramps, and such things. When she was 25 she married Fred, a long-distance truck driver, and lived with him when he was home and she was well. But each attack of pneumonia she suffered over the years left scars on her one good lung, and she developed emphysema that forced her to spend much of her life either in the hospital or recuperating in our living room. My children never resented the time I spent caring for Doris. She was just seven years older than Danny and they saw her more as a sister than an aunt.

We had many scares. One night while Danny was still at Jeff State he was working the switchboard and talking to Doris on the phone when she suddenly went silent. He set the system on automatic, and sped to her apartment where he found her unconscious and rushed her to the hospital. When he carried her into the emergency room an intern said, "Put her on the table. We'll get to her soon." Danny grabbed the intern and said, "You'll get to her right now." After that we all learned to call the doctor and have him admit her while we were on the way.

One time when Doris was critically ill, Mother and Esta came to Mt. Olive and let me drive them to the hospital. Doris was on a respirator and I wanted to prepare them for the sight. No one did that for me the first time I saw her unconscious on a big machine that was forcing her to breathe. I lived with that nightmare for a long time. So I was telling them about her condition and what they would see, and Mother suddenly said, "I've always felt guilty about what Bradley and I did to you children. I think that Doris is paying for what your father and I did." I was stunned. That was the only time I ever heard her admit that she had done anything wrong. I imagine she was referring to the passage in the Bible about the sins of the father being visited on the sons. I don't interpret that passage the way she did, but I agree that she had totally failed in her responsibilities toward her children and had hurt us beyond repair. By this time it was far too late to talk about it, though. I think I mumbled something like, "I'm glad to hear you admit that," and we remained silent the rest of the way to the hospital.

Doris spent her final months with us. She was now bedridden but didn't want to be in a room by herself; she wanted to be in the middle of the action. We put her in the corner of the living room on a day bed that we elevated by putting bricks under it. She was on oxygen around the clock, which meant we couldn't turn on our gas heaters, so we piled quilts on everyone. The sound of her jagged breathing radiated through the house and couldn't be ignored.

One morning when I was helping her use a bedpan, it seemed to me that she was having a seizure and starting to hallucinate. I told her I was taking her to the hospital.

"Don't take me to the hospital," she said. "I won't come back."

I felt, like she did, that the end was real close. I wanted to honor her wishes, but at that time Kathy, Nina, Cindy and Scott were at home. I couldn't handle having her die there with the children watching her, so I was determined to take her to the hospital if I could figure out how to get her there. I knew that if I called an ambulance she'd be extremely upset, but I'd have to be quick if I took her myself. We didn't have portable oxygen tanks at that time and she couldn't stay off of oxygen long. I got someone from the body shop across the street to help me load her in the car, then rushed to Carraway Hospital. The staff was familiar with her and put her immediately in intensive care, where she stayed all that day and night. I was able to get in touch with her husband, who came and stayed with her, and with Daddy, who said he was coming. The doctor told me it would be just a matter of time and for us not to leave the hospital.

"Will you tell that to her father when he gets here?" I asked. "He has a bad habit of not believing me."

The doctor said, "Just have them page me when he comes and I'll come talk to him." When Daddy arrived and saw Doris, he was visibly shaken. Afterward the doctor talked to him.

Calvin was there in his painter's clothes and left to go home, change, and take the girls to their ball game. Daddy suddenly decided to go home—to Berry. I said, "Daddy, the doctor has already told you it was just going to be a matter of hours."

"Well, they've been wrong before," he said and left. When she became comatose early the next morning we called him and he said he would come back that evening, but she died before he got there.

Danny was living in Atlanta when Calvin called to tell him that Doris had little time left. He hurried to his apartment, changed clothes, and flew down I-20 trying to get to Birmingham before she died. He told us that when he got to where the Talladega Speedway is now, Doris came to him. He didn't see her but felt her and thought he heard her say, "Slow down, I'm okay." He remembers looking at the time on his dashboard clock and finding out later that it matched the hour of her death on June 13, 1974.

Doris had many friends who came to her funeral. The family all came, and where they sat was a good representation of the relationships in our family. Mother and Esta sat in the audience, not with us. In the family section was her husband Fred, her brothers Milford and Karrold, Calvin and me and our five children, and her half-brothers and sisters by Clara. Daddy wouldn't go into the church; he sat in the preacher's office. ❧

This is Doris in my kitchen in the early 1970s with her two sisters, Esta, standing, and me.

Alarm

With Doris gone, Danny grown, Kathy getting ready to graduate from high school and only the three youngest needing tending to, it seemed that I was going to have more time for myself. I was doing a lot of quilting and was busy starting a quilter's guild at the Mt. Olive Community Center when I just ran out of steam. Part of it was the enormous workload I had, and I probably didn't eat as well as I should or take the vitamins I was supposed to. I went for a check-up and Dr. Whitten told me I was anemic and that my Pap smear did not look good. It wasn't cancerous but I should have another test in three months. He also called in my children and had them tested. They all turned out to be anemic, so he put the whole family on vitamins. Every meal became pill-passing time.

After the second Pap smear, Dr. Whitten's nurse, who was a friend of mine, called and said, "Dr. Whitten wants to talk to you." And he got on the phone and said, "Come in."

Well, I couldn't come in. My neighbor Betty Dobbs was in the hospital and I was taking care of her daughter Kandi, who was a year younger than Scott. When I told him that, he repeated, "Be here." He asked me what time Calvin got in and said, "I want both of you in here. You've got uterine cancer. I want you in the hospital tomorrow."

"I can't go," I answered. By this time, we weren't as close to Evelyn and Elmer as we had been and I didn't want to ask them to look after the kids.

"You will go or we'll come after you." He knew how pig-headed I was.

"I can't go until Betty Dobbs comes home so she can help take care of my children." After checking around I found that "MomBetty" was being released the next day and her mother was coming to stay with her, so I went in, knowing that Nina and Cindy could look after Scott until Betty's mother got there. Betty and I passed each other in the lobby of the hospital; she was going home as I came in.

Because of my past history I was supposed to have a complete hysterectomy but the surgeon decided to do a vaginal hysterectomy, which removes the uterus through the vagina instead of an incision. After the surgery I got a clean bill of health and needed no further treatments, but it took me a long time to bounce back. Summer wore on and I began to have an awful lot of pain in my right side. When I lay flat on my back I could feel a hard spot in my groin area. I had an uneasy feeling about it and lived with a looming fear, afraid to go to the doctor. Eight months after the original surgery, when it got so bad that I didn't have a choice, I went to Dr. Whitten, who ordered x-rays. They revealed a shadow or mass that he believed was cancer.

The next couple of weeks were the darkest days I've ever lived. All I could think of was dying before my children were grown. Danny and Kathy were both married and on their own. Though Nina and Cindy were in high school and old enough to take care of themselves, I wasn't ready to part with them. Scott was just eleven. I couldn't stand the thought of him being motherless or of Calvin marrying someone who would treat Scott like my stepmother had treated us. I spent many sleepless nights praying "Let me live just long enough to get him grown and big enough to take care of himself."

Meanwhile the specialists at the hospital had decided to do radiation, but I had a nagging feeling that radiation wasn't the right thing for me. I wanted to go home, collect my thoughts, and talk to my children before I consented to go through with it. Calvin shouldn't be the one to tell Nina, Cindy, and Scott I had cancer and I didn't want them to come to the hospital to hear it from me. I had just decided to pack up my things and have Calvin pick me up when Dr. Whitten walked in. He always wore cowboy boots and I could hear him coming up the hall. He looked at my chart then looked up at me and said, "I don't understand what's going on. Why are they going to do radiation and not surgery?"

"They aren't going to do radiation on me. I'm going to go home."

"They have you on the chart to start tomorrow."

I told him I wasn't going to let them cook me like a Christmas turkey. He called the nurse, examined me some more, then left the room for a while. When he came back he said, "You're going to have surgery."

"But they said they couldn't operate until they did radiation."

"They are going to operate in the morning at 7:00. You have Calvin here."

And at his insistence, they did surgery. Instead of cancer they found a hard, black mass. They determined that when the doctor did the vaginal hysterectomy, he bruised my right ovaries and blood had accumulated into a mass. There was no malignancy.

There have been a few easy times in my life, but there've been very few. It has mainly been a succession of hard times, with this being the hardest. But even then I wasn't at the point of hopelessness. My faith tells me that God has a reason for whatever happens. If I was meant to die of cancer, so be it. But it seemed that he meant for me to live and get all the children grown and on their own. ❧

Common Ground

*Calvin and I spent many summer hours coaching
girls' softball teams in Mt. Olive.*

Throughout all our troubles, Calvin and I agreed on one thing
above all. We wanted our children to get through school knowing
how to do something. I quit school to marry Calvin when I was in
the eighth grade and I always regretted the fact that I didn't have a
formal education. In school I had learned to read and write and do
a little arithmetic, and that's it. The rest of my education comes from
living, primarily from my experiences with Doris in the hospital,
from the organizations I've been involved with, and from just teaching myself to do what needed to be done. Calvin didn't get beyond
the eighth grade, either. His mother was not big on education and
would have been quite happy if none of her children ever did
anything but farm. She never encouraged them to stay in school; she

never encouraged them to get a job; she never encouraged her daughters to work or be creative. Theirs was a ho-hum way of life. They said to themselves, "This is it and this is as good as it gets." But Calvin and I got a different perspective when we moved away and saw how others lived. We were poor dumb little kids when we got married, but now we knew that our children needed more education than we had. So from the very beginning we told them, "You will get a good education. You will definitely finish school. If you don't want college, you'll have some kind of vocational training." And we were able to do that by the hardest.

As I was growing up I watched how real families acted and noticed that the parents of the best students were usually active in the school. So I went to PTA meetings and served as a perpetual room mother. Teachers in Mount Olive knew me and knew that the Kimbrell children were expected to get good grades and behave themselves or their parents would beat the squash out of them. I've seen too many parents who believe their children can do no wrong, but I've always been under the assumption that mine would do anything they thought they could get by with. They didn't because they knew that if they got in trouble at school, word would get back to Calvin or me and there would be more trouble waiting for them at home.

We figured the best way to keep them out of trouble was to be with them as much as possible. When we moved to Mount Olive, I joined the Baptist church there and all the children attended with me. Calvin would be at home on Sunday morning and he would tell them, "You are getting up and going with your mother to church," but he would stay home and listen to gospel music on the radio. That was his church.

Every summer I was in charge of the kitchen at vacation bible school. At that time we had a music director who thought he was God's gift to the world, I reckon. He was going to lay down guidelines and everyone in the church was going to follow them or be cast aside. We were in the kitchen one Monday morning and folks were talking about something that had occurred at church last night.

When I asked about it, the music director looked at me hard.

"Where were you that you weren't at church?"

"I was fishing."

You would have thought we had an earthquake under that kitchen.

"What do you mean you were fishing?"

I said, "Let me give you a scenario and you tell me whether I'm right or wrong. You know that Calvin does not go to church here. You take any family where the husband and wife both go on a regular basis—any one of the deacons. You follow them home from church. The husband's going to go off and play golf, or he's going to pile up on the sofa and watch a football game, or his kids are going to go skating or something. The wife's going to come back down here and do a tea or whatever. They have no family time. I took my kids and my husband and we spent the afternoon together in God's country on the river. Now tell me which one's the worst."

Woo, he got mad at me. He wouldn't speak to me for a long time after that because I put him on the spot. But he knew I was right. We were there as a family, understanding each other, communicating and having a good time.

The place you would find us together most often during summers was the Mt. Olive ballpark, which was within seeing and hearing distance of our house. For a great many years the community only sponsored baseball teams for boys. There was nothing for girls, so when Kathy was about ten, Calvin and I helped form a girl's softball league and started coaching. He also organized turkey shoots to raise money for bases, lights, dugouts, and equipment.

Calvin never had the opportunity to play sports as a boy, so he made sure his boys and girls got that chance—even if they weren't as enthusiastic about it as he was. When the league began, there was a wide age range on each team. Cindy, who was only five, was on my team with Kathy and Nina. Cindy, who lived and breathed sports, remembers Nina standing in right field fanning herself with her glove and asking "Can I go sit in the dug out? It's hot out here."

Calvin would tell Cindy, "You better not let that ball get past your sister." He expected her to run from center field to catch anything Nina missed. Often she did.

I had never played a team sport in my life, either. Everything I knew I learned by watching Danny's coaches when I took him to baseball practice. I wasn't one who would just open the car door, let my child out, say "Hey, what time are y'all going to be finished?" and drive off. I hung around to see if anything needed to be done. Some of us would clean the concession stand or pick up paper in the park or watch after the kids who had been dropped off. During Danny's baseball years I absorbed enough knowledge of the sport that I became a pretty good coach. I usually had winning girls' teams and the coaches of the boys' teams often asked me to be their scorekeeper.

When Scott first started playing, his team had to search for a coach. Ronnie, a young man from the community, volunteered for the job because two of his nephews wanted to play ball. The only problem was that Ronnie was known to be a drug user and dealer and had recently let a few people know that he was gay. Gayness wasn't something folks thought much about in those times. When they did, they didn't approve of it, but they didn't worry about it affecting them. I was more worried about him trying to hook the boys on drugs than coming on to them. I didn't want a controversy in the community, however, and decided to handle it quietly.

At the first practice a deputy sheriff drove up and said, "What is that S.O.B. doing out there with those kids?"

"He's the coach."

"Do you know what he does?" I said I did and would keep an eye on him.

"You'd better watch him close. If you have any problem at all, call me and I'll be right there."

When practice was over I went up to him and introduced myself to him as Scott's mother and the self-appointed team mother. I told him, "When you come to practice, you don't bring anything but the equipment. I will have their drinks, towels and anything else they need. Don't you bring anything in this dugout; if you do, it's going out. When we get to a ball game, I will be your scorekeeper; I will be your organizer. I'm going to be right here. As far as I'm concerned no other mother is going to know what you are into. But I promise you that if I see one thing out of the way, I'll use one of these ball bats on you. You'll know I've been here. That's my child and you will not mess with him." And he didn't.

Years later, when Calvin and I celebrated our 45th anniversary at the community center, Ronnie was in the receiving line. When he got up to me he said, "Do you know what's wrong with so many kids running around these days? They never had someone like you to make them behave."

When the ball season was over, the turkey shoots would begin. Turkey shoots were a common way for an organization like a VFW lodge or volunteer fire department to raise money. Turkeys were the prizes, not the prey. The one Calvin ran every Saturday for more than ten years was well known. People would arrive at daylight from as far away as Georgia and Tennessee. Calvin set up twelve targets and passed out shotgun shells to each person who paid $5 or $10 to shoot in that round. The best shot won a frozen turkey, a ham, a block of cheese, a hunk of bologna, a case of oranges, or a cash prize. Turkey shoots were guy things and I didn't go to them. Most of the men who came didn't care how much money they spent or what they won, they just wanted to shoot their guns. Some would stay there all day, shooting as many as 20 rounds, so the turkey shoots were lucrative for the ballpark. Calvin took no money for running them, but Danny says his dad cleaned up on side bets. Nobody told me about those at the time.

During the school year my job was to be the stay-at-home mom, the one who ends up making cookies for bake sales and being chaperone on field trips and the unpaid provider of after-school care. When the school bus stopped at our house, half of its passengers unloaded. One day Cindy asked, "Why is it that every stray child and every stray dog likes our house best?" I had no idea how many would get off that bus on a given day. There'd be Betty

Dobbs' three kids from across the street plus three or four others whose mothers had told them to come over here in the afternoon because they weren't going to be home. The elementary school principal's granddaughter would come and stay until her grandfather picked her up after he finished for the day. I always had something—brownies or Rice Krispies squares—freshly baked and sitting on the counter. The kids would pile into our house until the walls bowed, throw their book bags on the floor, and head for the kitchen. Then they'd go out into the yard to play.

There was potential for things to get out of hand but we didn't let that happen. Cindy was at a cookout a few years ago and a childhood friend said, "I swore I would not raise my kids like I was raised. My parents never whipped me and I was so rotten. The only whippings I got were from Cindy's parents."

Everybody seemed surprised. "Why did they whip you?"

"Because we were playing in their front yard. And if a fight broke out in the front yard and you were in the front yard you'd get a whipping."

Calvin told the kids to tell their parents to come see him if they had a problem with his style of punishment. But no kid wanted to be banished from our yard and the ones who got whippings never failed to come back the next day. I've always thought it was better to stop bad behavior as soon as it happened than to let it grow and then say "I can't handle this. You kids go away and don't come back."

Calvin and I didn't know how to use psychology; we punished the way we were punished as children. One of the stories the kids loved for Calvin to tell shows the kind of punishment he was used to. His daddy didn't allow any talking at the table. You came to the table to eat and when you were done, you left the table. Their table was a long one with two benches that held all nine kids. At supper one night Calvin said he got to talking about something that had happened at school. His daddy said, "I told you, boy, to quit talking at the table." Calvin got quiet but then remembered a detail he'd left out and started talking again. His father reached over the table and backhanded him.

"When I woke up," Calvin would say, "I was on the floor staring at the ceiling and my legs were hanging over the bench. Everybody else was just sitting at the table eating like nothing was going on."

I was not so sudden with my punishments, but I was not afraid to use a switch. When I took my children to town, even the little country town of Gardendale, I expected them to behave. If they didn't I might grab an ear, lean over, and whisper, "When we get home, you are getting a spanking." Scott says he could grow a halo and some really pretty golden wings, carry groceries for me and the lady beside me, help me unload the groceries, and then be out on his bicycle playing an hour after we got home and I would come to the door and say, "I need for you to come in for a minute."

"Yeah, Mom, what do you need?"

"You remember that whipping I promised you?"

"Yeah."

"Well here it comes." I was like Mama in those regards, but I tried to be fair and the children knew I was training them to do right. Scott says that as the youngest one it was easier for him to behave because he could see what the older ones did and what they got as a result. ✢

Fishing was the big pastime for us on Sundays after church. In the photo on the right Scotty is showing off a fish he caught.

Daughters

My three little girls, from top to bottom: Kathy, Nina, and Cindy

This is what I wanted for my children: First, that they grow up in a happy, secure home and, second, that they have the opportunity to explore their lives and choose who and what they wanted to be before they married. I did not want them forced into lives they did not like because they had to support babies too soon. When I had Danny at age 14 I was ready for him, but I wanted something different for my children.

I didn't have anybody to show me how to achieve that and there was certainly no grand revelation in the night that spelled out a plan for me in glittering letters. But I figured out that if my children were involved in church, school, and sports activities, there would be a better chance of their careers, love, marriage, and children coming in the right order. So Calvin and I participated in their activities and kept a tight rein on them, especially the girls. As young children they loved our closeness but as each of our daughters became teenagers, they rebelled. Oh did they rebel.

Calvin didn't let boys come around his three pretty girls nor did we let them go riding around with carloads of teenagers or spend the night at girlfriends' houses. If we did, how could we keep an eye on them? Our girls continuously complained that they weren't allowed to do what everyone else at Mortimer Jordan High School did. Kathy says we must have believed that if she wore make up or shaved her legs like the other girls, she was on the fast track to being a harlot.

Kathy

Even though she complained about our strictness, Kathy was the easiest of the three girls. She was our family scholar who always pushed herself toward academic excellence, made mostly A's, and was in the National Honor Society. During her senior year, 1975, she didn't apply for any prestigious colleges or any major scholarships—we didn't know how to do such things—but she got a scholarship to Jefferson State Community College and for the next two years she studied and worked on campus and lived at home, where she had to follow our rules. She felt smothered here and asked if she could move into an apartment with a girlfriend who needed a roommate.

"Your dad is never going to go for that," I told her.

She struggled to get up the nerve to talk to Calvin about it, and when she finally did, he threw a fit. He stomped around the living room and yelled," I will see you in your coffin before you move out of this house." She believed him. You know the saying "I brought you into the world and I can take you out of it?" Kathy says that her dad had a way of making you think he'd take you out of the world real quick.

So she remained at home and had no trouble getting her associate degree in English. When graduation time came, Calvin called his mother and asked her to come up for a couple of days because Kathy was the only grandchild she would ever see graduate from college, which turned out to be true. I was sure Kathy would go on to a university, but it turned out that while she was working at Jeff State she met a campus policeman and had been going out with him on the sly. She was 20 and ready to marry Dennis, the only man she had ever dated. I made her wedding dress and at her request we had the reception at our house, which got its first air-conditioner for the occasion. Soon after, she and Dennis moved to Louisiana for awhile, had two sons, and eventually came back to Mt. Olive.

Nina

Nina left home because of our strictness. She graduated from high school in 1979 shortly after my cancer episode. She had never been good at academics, but she was talented with her hands. She always tried whatever I was doing, like crocheting and quilting, and she made big wardrobes for her Barbie dolls. When she cleaned house for Mrs. Russell in exchange for music instruction, she would go into her yard and gather flowers for bouquets. Mrs. Russell encouraged her to be a florist, a suggestion that proved more fruitful than the piano lessons did. When it came time to choose a trade in high school, Nina signed up for floriculture, design with flowers. She took academic classes in the morning and for school credit worked at a plant nursery in the afternoons and on weekends. By the time she graduated, she was a good arranger with a flair for the exotic and worked at David Mitchell's flower shop in Gardendale. About this time her headstrong nature ran straight up against mine. David Mitchell, besides being a florist, raised greyhounds and raced them at the new dog track in Greene County, about ninety miles west of Gardendale. David's daughter Debbie worked at the shop and introduced Nina to some boys who worked at the track with her father. Nina wanted to go out there but I wouldn't let her. Being a good Baptist, I don't go in too much for gambling. It's contrary to God's word, the way I read it. And Calvin just didn't want her to be anywhere but home. Nina thought it was unfair that she had graduated from high school without ever having a date. She tried to talk Calvin into letting her go out but he dug in. Like Kathy, Nina was afraid of him. He had never physically hurt her but had a temper bad enough that it scared the tar out of her.

A friend of Nina knew how tight Calvin was on the girls and told Nina she would probably need to move out if she ever wanted to date. After a lot of agonizing, she made up her mind and called me.

"When I get off work, me and Debbie's going to the race track with these two guys."

"Well, don't come home. You know what the rules are. As long as you live in my house and put your feet under my table, you'll abide by the rules."

"I just won't come home."

She had a car that we had helped her get. I said, "Well, leave the car.

You can't take the car."

So Nina moved in with a family in Gardendale and never came back. I was so mad at her for disobeying me that I'm not sure I wanted her back. Calvin began to soften but we had an agreement that we would support each other in disciplining the children, so he didn't interfere. I was less forgiving than Calvin; I guess I inherited that from Mama. I told Nina, "I've done all I can do as a parent. What you do with yourself from here on out is up to you." I knew that if I hadn't made an impression on her and taught her right from wrong by then, there wasn't any point in starting now. I had to let go and it hurt. It cost me a lot of sleep. I'd lie in bed wondering if I was wrong and reevaluating the way I had raised her.

We stayed angry at each other for only a month or so, but she didn't move back home. By the time we had ended our standoff she had met Mark and one night called to say she wanted to marry him.

Calvin asked, "Does he have long hair?" He didn't. When we met Mark, a carpenter and homebuilder, we got along with him and soon Calvin was walking Nina down the aisle. Now Nina and Mark and I are so close I can't think of anything that would ever drive a wedge between us.

Cindy

Cindy's early departure was the most traumatic for us. We should have predicted it would happen, but she and Calvin were two of a kind and so close most of the time that we didn't see it coming.

Like Calvin, she was a prankster. How she got through school without being expelled, God only knows. I guess the officials knew that everything Cindy did was in fun, with no malice or disrespect intended. She was full of life and part of any pranks that were being played in Mt. Olive. If I passed by a yard with toilet paper hanging down from the trees, I knew she had been in on the "rolling," as they called it. If I heard that a P.E. teacher was thrown in the shower with her clothes on, I assumed that Cindy had been the ringleader.

Unlike her sisters, Cindy wasn't afraid of Calvin. One day she and Kandi Dobbs sneaked out of her bedroom window and wrapped my brother's truck in toilet paper while Calvin and he were sitting in the living room. When Karrold opened the front door to leave he said "Somebody rolled my truck."

Calvin said, "I bet I know who did it." He turned around to go in the house and Cindy and Kandi, who were hiding behind the truck, took off toward Cindy's bedroom window. Cindy had planned to dive in and be sitting on the bed when he came in the room. She would innocently say, "Hey Daddy, what's up?" But Calvin got there in time to see Cindy on her bed and Kandi with one leg in the window and one leg out. It was hard for Calvin not to laugh as he disciplined them.

"Y'all need to get out in the yard and clean that toilet paper up. Tomorrow you are going to the store and buy your mother some more toilet paper."

"Yes, sir."

When Calvin was drunk she was foolhardy, and we all worried about her. I stayed out of their arguments but Cindy could see me standing in the kitchen and read my face and my gestures.

He would walk in the front door and yell, "Get these shoes out of the living room—if I have to tell you one more time. . ."

Cindy would say, "Well, your shoes are here too. Why are you yelling at us?"

He'd roar, "Don't you back talk me."

"Well there's a pair of your shoes here and. . ." I would gesture for her to stop right now and yank my thumb toward her room. If we were lucky, she would follow it.

She loved to test him. When Calvin would send Cindy to the refrigerator to get him a beer she would snap back with something like "I'm not a barmaid." She would get it for him, but one time she stayed in the kitchen and shook it as hard as she could. When it spewed all over him he asked, "Did you shake this?" and she answered with a straight face, "No, it must have fallen out of the refrigerator." Another time when he was talking on the phone, which he did a lot, she picked up his cigarette lighter and rolled the flame all the way up, then stayed there watching TV until Calvin lighted a cigarette and almost burned his nose off.

"Did you turn that up?"

Cindy said "No" and looked at me, reading my eyes saying, "You are going to get your butt torn off."

Her temperament was so much like Calvin's it was like two flint rocks when they got together. During her teenage years and his hard drinking years, Cindy and Calvin argued religiously to the point of almost coming to blows three or four times a week. Scott hated it. He'd complain, "Nobody's arguing in the entire house but those two."

Some of their best times and worst times were at the ballpark. If she hit a home run and brought in three other runners, he'd yell, "That's my girl. That's what I'm talking about." Maybe the next inning the other team would hit one to right field and Nina would miss it. If Cindy didn't get behind her fast enough, he would take her by her collar, lift her off the ground up to eye level with him and say, "If you let another one get past your sister, I'm going to tear your tail up." Cindy says the next time she went to bat—still furious at him—she'd hear him yell, "You'd better get a hit." Her anger would make her swing so hard that sometimes she would slam the ball out of the park. That was part of his strategy, she thinks.

It hurts to tell about her leaving home, but I can do it because it led to something good. Cindy was a senior in high school, and Calvin was deeper into whiskey than ever. One evening she was on the phone and when Calvin said he needed to use it, she smarted off to him. To everyone's amazement, he backhanded her. The blow broke her nose and pushed her glasses back into her cheekbones, giving her two black eyes. The next morning at breakfast he looked at her and said, "Sis, what happened to you?"

"You hit me," she yelled.

"I don't remember doing that."

At that moment she hated him. She insisted on going to school in that condition, probably to embarrass him. One of the teachers found out what happened and told her, "I have to report this. I know that your daddy did this. It's abuse."

Cindy said, "If you do, they are going to arrest him, and my mother doesn't have enough money to get him out of jail. Please don't do it."

"Cindy, I have to; it's the law and if I don't report it, I could lose my job."

"If I leave home today and don't go back, will you not do it?"

Cindy had a close friend, Tootie Henderson, whose mother had seen the way Calvin acted at the ballpark. She told Cindy several times that if she ever got tired of the way he treated her, she could come live with them. Cindy thought she'd never do that but at the moment it seemed a good solution to the problem.

"You have to promise me that you won't go home. I want you to call and get someone to come check you out of school because if you go back home and he hurts you, it's on my head."

In front of her teacher Cindy called Mrs. Henderson, crying, and said, "Will you come and get me?" Cindy says that the next phone call was the hardest phone call she ever made. Calvin was away hunting and when she gave me the news I said, "Oh honey, don't do that. Please don't do that. It almost killed Calvin when Nina left home. He didn't mean to hurt you. I won't let him lay a hand on you again. Please tell me where you are. I'll come get you. We won't tell Daddy this even happened."

"I'm not coming home."

"He's going to go crazy." She said she didn't have a choice.

I went to the country to get Calvin and tell him what happened. He drove back and went door-to-door in the neighborhood looking for her. Cindy says that someone called Mrs. Henderson and told her he had come to their door looking for Cindy and didn't need to find her because he was in a bad way. She told Cindy and Tootie to get in the car, drive around another part of town, and call after an hour to see if it was safe to come home. Cindy remembers stopping at a pay phone and learning that Calvin had been there and gone. She returned to the Hendersons and settled in, then called and said she needed her clothes and shoes. I put them in garbage bags on the front porch for her to pick up at a time I knew Calvin wouldn't be there.

Calvin agonized over the loss of Cindy. She made him see what his drinking was doing to the people he loved, and he simply stopped. When Cindy called me I would tell her, "You need to come home. He's different. He's not drinking whiskey. He's not even drinking beer." But she was still afraid to come home.

I did not like the Hendersons and I worried about the home life Cindy would have there, but I knew that she would be safe at school. All five of my children went to Mortimer Jordan High School. The principal respected Calvin and I, and I knew he would let nothing happen to Cindy. Mr. Trotter called her into his office and said, "I understand your situation, that you aren't living at home. If you need anything—lunches paid for, senior pictures, graduation invitations— we will get them and if you want to reimburse me when you graduate and go to work, you can. But we want you to stay in school and graduate."

Scott was in junior high on the same campus, so Cindy sent her graduation invitation home by him with a note inside that I still have. She wrote, "I love y'all very much. Graduation is finally here and there is nothing in the world I would love any better than for y'all to please come. It's taken me 12 years to finally do it and God knows I couldn't have done it without y'all's help, love, and guidance. Please come."

Calvin, still hurt and angry, said we wouldn't attend. For once I went against him. Cindy remembers sitting at graduation in her cap and gown and looking up in the stands for her family. She was so happy when she saw Scott and me but when she went looking for us afterward, we were not there. I wanted to see her but didn't need a confrontation with the Henderson family, so we slipped out quickly.

A family trip to Baton Rouge brought Cindy back into the fold. Kathy and Dennis had moved there after their wedding and Calvin, Scott and I were going to visit her for a week. We invited Cindy, but she was still unsure. She hadn't seen Calvin in almost a year and was worried that it would just be a week of fighting that she couldn't escape. Finally, on the day we were leaving, she called and said, "Come and get me and I'll go with y'all."

Calvin was Fun-Daddy the whole week. He and Cindy didn't discuss the situation but on the way home, when we got almost to Mt. Olive, he said, "Sis, You are 18. I can't tell you what to do, but I'm ready for you to come home. I wish you would consider coming home." And she remembers thinking, "Oh thank God." She had wanted to be home the whole time.

When Cindy went to get her clothes, Mrs. Henderson was furious. She said that we were luring her into our web and Calvin was going to hit her again. "That's what abusive parents do," she said. But Calvin wasn't drinking any more and Cindy knew that things were going to be okay. When she decided to marry Jerry, a young man we had known for years, she set her wedding date on Calvin's birthday. ❧

Sunshine

Since I was a child I knew I wanted my future children to finish school knowing how to do something. When Scott graduated in 1987, I was thrilled that Calvin and I and all five of them had made that happen.

There's an old song that goes "The sun's going to shine in my back door some day. March wind's going to blow my blues all away." So far I'd had a lot of trouble in my life and I was beginning to think that hard work and frustration were all I would ever know. But happiness somehow managed to circle around to the back of the house and sneak in. That happened when Calvin stopped drinking and started staying at home with me.

Our last 15 years together were rewards for all the troubles that we'd had. The traumas with Danny and the girls were settled and we'd paid off the house and car loans. We still didn't have any money, but we were comfortable with our finances and with each other. I can't really explain how we made it to this point, but somehow we escaped divorce and returned to the relationship we'd had in the beginning.

Scott was the only child still at home. He was my unwanted pregnancy that turned into the son any mother would want. He did not excel as a student but he was good-looking, athletic, and clean cut. I never had to check and see if he was slipping out and smoking. He made sure I knew where he was and what he was doing. He and Cindy were polar opposites. When he would tell me he was going to the church to shoot baskets, Cindy says that she would think "Yeah, right. I can't believe Mama's falling for that," because that was what she would say when she was going some forbidden place. To catch him in a lie, she would wait a while and tell me that she was going to the store for a minute. She would drive by the church and, son of a gun, there he'd be, shooting baskets.

Cindy, besides being mischievous and athletic, was also artistic. If I needed a special design for one of my quilts I'd ask, "Can you draw me a little rose or daisy with a vine to go right here?" and she would. It was easy for her to choose her field in vocational school. She took commercial arts classes and has had good jobs as a graphic artist since she graduated.

Scott planned to go to college and didn't take vocational courses at school. When he graduated, however, he couldn't decide on a field to major in. By this time Kathy and Dennis had moved back to Mt. Olive and she was administrative assistant to the chairman of the Psychology Department at the University of Alabama in Birmingham. She told Scott that she had seen too many kids wasting their time and money in college when they didn't know what they were there for. A friend of ours who worked at a large printing company in Birmingham told him about an opening as an assistant to a pressman there and suggested that Scott take it while he decided what he wanted to do. He has been there since the day he applied and now is the lead six-color pressman.

Scott's wedding day in 1991 marked the first time in 40 years that there were no children living with Calvin and me. The little ones I had dreamed of and vowed to love and provide for since I was ten years old now had families of their own. But the house never felt empty because they and their children were always dropping in to eat and to help around the house. Calvin was having health problems and wasn't working any more, so he was there to play with Cindy's son Brian while she was at work. And he was a master at getting fresh vegetables for us to can.

After Nina had her first child, Jake, she decided to give up her job as a florist and stay home with him, meaning that money was short for her family. Since she had grown up canning, she decided to save money by putting up a lot of her own food. She came over every day during the summer, brought Jake to play with Brian, and the two of us canned vegetables. Friends would call and offer produce from their gardens and Calvin would say, "Yeah, we need it. I'll be right there." He would come in with loads of produce that people had given him. We had vegetables stacked up in the kitchen, on the floor of the living room, everywhere. Nina kept saying "We're never going to get caught up." We wore ourselves out that summer, but talked all winter about how good the food was and how little it cost.

When Nina was ready to work outside the home again she joined with a caterer, and the two would do flowers, decorations, and food for events, mainly weddings. They got me to bake and ice wedding cakes, and Nina would festoon them with live flowers. One afternoon I was icing a cake and the icing was not cooperating. I got thoroughly frustrated trying to smooth it down. Calvin was a master drywall man who could return a beat-up wall to perfection with a putty knife in very short time. He was watching me from his chair in the living room and thinking to himself, "I have smoothed sheet rock with the finest of the fine, so I can definitely do that frosting." He said, "Bett, if you go get that 10-inch sheetrock knife out of the garage and clean it up, I'll fix it for you."

"I bought a new one yesterday," I said, " and it's right here."

I sat everything out on the corner of the table and left the room. When I came back in he was sitting in his chair studying that cake.

"What's wrong?"

"That damn stuff don't act like sheetrock mud."

It was fun having Calvin at home. I guess it would be normal for me to resent him for all those years that he let me bear most of the burdens of caring for Doris and raising the children while he spent money we couldn't afford on drinking and other women. But I couldn't hold on to my resentment when he so obviously regretted doing those things. It was not a verbal thing. Calvin, like many men of his time, couldn't talk about relationships and couldn't say "I love you" or "I'm sorry for the pain I caused you." However, he wore those feelings on his face. The kids and I forgave him and were thrilled to have the real Calvin Kimbrell back. ❧

Community

Photo courtesy of the *North Jefferson News*

Proceeds from the North Jefferson Quilter's Guild annual quilt show paid most of the bills for the Mt. Olive Community Center. This was taken at the fourth annual show in 1983.

One constant, besides my faith, accompanied me through the dark days as well as the sunny ones. I had taken up quilting with new passion after my blue ribbon from the state fair in 1970 and I stitched my way through trials by cancer, rebellious daughters, and a wayward husband. In the midst of these tribulations my quilting took on a new aspect. I became a public quilter.

This started in 1972 when the federal government turned over the old Mt. Olive School to the Jefferson County Commission to use as a community center. It was a tall wood frame building with wide halls, high ceilings, wooden floors, four big classrooms, and a combination gym and auditorium that could be used for basketball games, exercise classes, family reunions, and concerts. A small lunchroom and kitchen were attached to the back of the building and in 1976 this became a senior citizen's center and nutrition site sponsored by the County. A bus left the center every day to pick up elderly men and women and bring them there to socialize and have a hot meal. Calvin and I knew folks in Mt. Olive who were pretty much homebound because they never learned how to drive or couldn't drive any more. Some couldn't get to the store for groceries and some didn't even have a cup of coffee at home in the morning because they didn't want to make just one cup. We thought the senior citizen's program was a wonderful thing because it gave those people a reason to get up in the morning. Calvin was still working at the time, but when he was off he loved to visit with the folks there and help in any way he could.

Before I knew what happened, I was involved in it up to my ears, mainly in raising money to keep the doors open. It seems that the county only paid for the food and staff of the nutrition program; the community center, run by volunteers, had to provide the air conditioning, telephone, water, toilet paper, and other things the senior citizens needed, plus pay for upkeep on the old building. The board of directors of the center continually put on last-minute fundraisers just to pay the utility bills. Because I'd worked with PTA and vacation Bible school and other things like that, someone on the board asked me to help with the 1978 fall carnival they were sponsoring. At the planning meeting they talked about bobbing for apples and having all the usual carnival games. I had put some thought into what I wanted to do, so when it was my turn I told them I would organize a quilt show. I had been quilting intensely for the last eight years, but I didn't know anything about quilt shows other than what I'd read in magazines and seen at the state fair. I wanted to try one, though. They asked me where I was going to get the quilts and I said, "I know enough people in this community who quilt that we can do it. Just give me a room and I'll get the quilts."

With board approval for the quilt show, I gathered up 50 or 60 quilts contributed by about eight women. We put the exhibit together in one day and did not hang them professionally nor award ribbons. It was simply a display for the public to enjoy. But our donation basket raised as much money as the other activities did, and we were proud of ourselves.

That little show was the seed of the North Jefferson Quilter's Guild that was born in 1980 and eventually became as much a part of my life as Calvin and the kids. It started with a suggestion from a member of the Birmingham Quilters Guild that we start one in Mt. Olive. At first I wasn't interested but after giving it more thought I decided it would be nice for women, and any men who so wished, to get together once a month to talk about quilts and to trade patterns. The community center board said we could meet there for free if we would help them raise money each year. When we started making quilts to raffle at fund-raisers we realized that once a month wouldn't suffice. We began meeting once a week, but when we started a night group for the working women, I found myself at the community center every Monday night and back there again on Tuesday morning. Our little exhibit at the fall carnival grew each year until it was a three-day quilt show that filled the gymnasium and most of the classrooms with quilted things—wall hangings, clothing, crafts, and, of course, quilts. With the proceeds from the quilt shows and raffles we were able to pay most of the bills for the community center.

Shortly after we started the guild, the president of the board of the community center died in a car wreck and I was elected to take his place. Now I was head of both the guild and the Mount Olive Community Center.

The more the guild grew, the more of my time it consumed. At first Calvin resented the time I was putting into it. He didn't like anything that kept me away from home and he'd say, "It ain't going to amount to a hill of beans. You're just wasting your time. You ought to be home doing something else." I dealt with that for a few years until he began to realize "Hey, we're on to something here."

And we were. We had our first quilt show in the fall of 1979 and formed the guild at a time when people across the country were getting interested in quilts again. I think people's taste for old-timey things had been whetted during the bicentennial celebrations in 1976. About the time we were getting started, a presidential commission announced that quilting was a national folk art and the postal service put out a series of stamps with quilt patterns on them. Curators at art museums started gathering up quilts and putting them on display.

Even our local weekly newspaper got caught up in quilting. In 1988 David Haynes, the editor of the *North Jefferson News*, called me and said he wanted to do a six-week series of articles that would tell readers how to make a quilt. When it was finished he would have an exhibit of all the quilts that had been made following my directions, and he would offer prizes. It would start in January, he said, because he wouldn't have anything else to write about after football season was over. I agreed to do it and suggested that instead of a quilt it should be a fairly simple wall hanging, about 35" square, so folks quilting for the first time would actually be able to finish it. That project was good for me. Sometimes as I was describing the next step he would say, "Hold on, explain to me what you are talking about." Then he would write it in a way that everyone could understand. I was surprised when thirteen good wall hangings were turned in at the end of the series.

Later the head of the art department at Jefferson State Community College called to see if I was interested in teaching quilting there. She wanted to offer credit courses that students could use to fulfill their humanities and fine arts requirements. She knew that not all Jeff State students were academically inclined. A good percentage of the students already had families, jobs, and a lot of commitments. They were returning to school to go into a different field or improve their earning potential. If you were going into nursing and had two young kids at home, and you had to hire a babysitter so you could go to school two days a week, you might not be real interested in Van Gogh and Mozart.

She told me she wanted to offer a quilting class but didn't have sewing machines. "Judy, I don't need sewing machines to teach," I replied. "All I need is a room and some tables."

"We've got that," she said.

So I became a professor of quilting. I designed pieces that could be done in a ten-week course, helped the students do them, and graded them on their efforts. I didn't expect perfection. For instance, if a seam was a little wider than it should be, I'd say, "This is not quite right." But unlike Mama, I wouldn't make them tear it out. I'd say, "Does it bother you?" If they said no, I'd say, "Leave it alone. You know that it's wrong and this is the way you should have done it, but if it's not going to bother you, leave it alone. And then the next time, do it this way." During the four years I taught there I tried to make quilting enjoyable for them, something they would want to do after the class was over. Ninety-nine percent of them left there planning another project, so I felt I accomplished something, and that little check at the end of the class helped Calvin and me pay the bills.

Meanwhile the North Jefferson Quilter's Guild had grown from a few Mt. Olive women meeting once a month into a large group of active quilters meeting twice a week. Folks were coming from all over the county to learn different quilting techniques, to get help with their own quilts, and to work on group quilts that we raffled off or gave to seriously ill children in the hospital. At any given meeting of the guild you would see women and an occasional man gathered around one or two quilt frames finishing up the raffle quilts, while across the hall would be several members working on a friendship quilt and others gathered around a table cutting out patchwork pieces. Or perhaps everyone would be focused on one member or a guest instructor showing them a particular quilting technique such as trapunto or appliqué. Of course we chatted while we sewed and we knew as much about everyone's families and circumstances as they wanted us to know. We went through illnesses and deaths together and prayed for each other and cried for each other and went to hospitals and funeral homes for each other. So the quilter's guild came to be about a lot more than quilting.

When I got into it I had no idea I'd be at the community center twice a week with the guild. It took a lot of dedication to commit six hours a week to an organization, plus answer all the phone calls I got from quilters all hours of the day and night, but I never resented the time I spent there. If I am helping somebody, I feel like that's what the Lord wants me to be doing. If I hadn't done it, I suppose someone else would have. We had excellent quilters in the guild that could teach as well as I did, but I did it because I wanted to, because the guild had become sacred to me. So I just let the dust get a little thicker at home and left some chores undone.

It paid off whenever someone like Patty showed up. Patty had two young daughters and chose to stay at home with them, even though it meant that she and her husband couldn't afford as nice a home as her friends had. She said some of her friends abandoned her because she couldn't keep up with them financially. But Patty had time to do some things they couldn't do, and one of those was to quilt. So on Monday nights, when her husband could watch after the girls, she took a class in strip-piecing the Lone Star pattern. That's a pattern that can be pieced together on a sewing machine better than by hand.

Patty had never used a sewing machine before. She had her strips cut and grouped together and I sat down at the sewing machine to show her how to place her material so she would have a quarter-inch seam allowance, and how to hold it to keep it aligned. I put a piece of tape a quarter of an inch from the needle and showed her how to slide her fabric along the edge of the tape, which would give her an exact seam allowance and keep her fabric from wiggling. I sewed the first two strips together and I put the material in the right position for the second seam and said, "Now you sew." She sat down at the machine and froze. "I can't do this. I'm going to tear. . ."

I said, "Patty, it's my sewing machine. I got it at a yard sale. If we tear it up, we'll fix it."

She looked up at me and her eyes said, "I can't do this."

"If you don't mash that foot and sew, I'm going to slap you." So she did. When she finished that line, she looked at me and said, "I sewed." It was just like I had given her a gift. She has gone on and bought herself a sewing machine and still quilts, as far as I know. The opportunity to share my knowledge with someone who desires it so much makes up for every Monday night and every Tuesday morning that I dragged myself there when I didn't feel like it, such as during my hard times with cancer, Calvin, and three teenage daughters. But those were the times I needed the friendship of quilters most.

That was the thing that Calvin had trouble understanding at first. He had never shared me before and he resented the hours I was gone. But then he began to see that it was good for the community and that other people were benefiting from it. Eventually he became as much a part of the group as any of us. He didn't quilt, but he made display racks for our shows. He was the security guard for our night meetings and after he retired there never was a Tuesday morning that he didn't drop in for a visit. He'd be out picking up garbage or doing some other chore, but he'd come down the hall and speak to everybody. He knew all the ladies by first name and he took time out to sit and talk to each one of them about their gardens and whatever else they were doing. He was a crucial part of the guild for 10 years.

Being responsible for a big old wooden schoolhouse, its plumbing, siding, landscaping, et cetera, wasn't much fun, but someone had to take charge and I got pretty fearless about making things happen. Early one morning Amy Brake, who ran the senior program, called to say that the center had been burglarized. I called the local police department and was told an officer would be at the center right away, so I drove there immediately. No policeman came, however, and after waiting two and a half hours I decided to go to the police station myself. As I turned out of the parking lot I saw a cop car at the diner next door. I went in just as the policeman was being served his bacon and eggs and told him he was supposed to be at the center. He said he would go there as soon as he finished his breakfast. That flew all over me. I pulled his plate away and said, "You'll do it right now. I've been down there waiting for you for two and a half hours." Everybody got real quiet. Another member of the community center was there and said, "I don't know if you know who she is, but if I was you I'd get up right now and file that police report." He did. ❧

Photo courtesy of the *North Jefferson News*

These women, seated at a quilting frame at the Mt. Olive Community Center, are finishing up a friendship quilt. Each square is signed by the guild member who made it (1989).

Quilts

Photo courtesy of the *North Jefferson News*

*My quilt, "Our Constitution," was included in an exhibit that
toured the Appalachian region. This photo was taken in 1987
when it came to the Hall of History in Bessemer, Alabama.*

When I wasn't teaching at Jeff State or the community center, decorating cakes, or spending time in Fayette County with family, I was quilting for myself—stacks of quilts, closets full of quilts, patchwork, appliqué, whole cloth—always trying out new designs and techniques.

In 1975 Danny's wife Denise read about a contest that the National Grange was sponsoring to celebrate the nation's bicentennial the next year. Doris had recently died and Denise thought the contest would capture my interest and help ease my grief. So I sat down and came up with a patchwork design made up of twelve blocks that looked like Betsy Ross's 1776 flag with its red and white stripes and thirteen blue stars. I alternated those with white squares filled with hand-stitched outlines of eagles and stars. I can look at that design now and see how little I knew about fine quilting at the time, but it won first place for Alabama and was part of the big exhibit at the Grange's national headquarters. I plan to give this one to Danny to honor his military service.

I continued making all sorts of quilts to please myself and about ten years later I did another quilt with a specific contest in mind. The Southern Highlands Craft Guild announced that it was going to have an exhibit in 1987 celebrating the 200th anniversary of the Constitution. My three daughters, all now in their twenties, helped me with that one. We sat down one day with the contest guidelines in hand and brainstormed. I told them "When I think about quilting I go back to Mama, her in her rocking chair." We designed a quilt that had at its center the figure of a woman in a rocking chair holding a small wooden embroidery hoop. In the hoop was a miniature quilt made of 20 squares, because Mama's quilts always had 20 patches. Each tiny square had an eight-point star in the center. I left a needle and thread in her quilt because the grandmother was still working on it. Above her head I embroidered "We, the quilters of the Appalachian region, in order to make known and preserve the art of quilting as a part of our heritage, seek to share in the celebration of the 200th Anniversary of the Constitution of the United States of America." Kathy helped me write that. When the top was finished, I quilted it in a simple shell pattern, which was the one that Mama always used. That quilt won best of show for the Alabama quilts and became part of an exhibit that toured all of the states throughout the Appalachian region for three years with 12 other quilts.

The rest of my quilts weren't done for any reason other than to try out different techniques, such as appliqué. Appliqué is French for "apply" and to appliqué a quilt top you cut cloth into shapes, fold their edges under and apply them to the base in a way that no one can see how they are attached. "Stained glass" quilts were popular in the 1980s. They usually imitated church windows, with designs made out of jewel-toned fabrics appliquéd to the quilt top and edged with strips of thin black fabric that represent the leading that connects individual pieces of stained glass into one image. Cindy drew up cheerful designs for me—flowers, birds, butterflies, Sun Bonnet Sue and Sam—twenty in all, and each one became the centerpiece of one of the panes in a very bright fabric window.

And I taught myself to do shadow trapunto. That's a type of

whole-cloth quilt, meaning the top and back are each made from one large piece of fabric. In traditional trapunto, you stitch a design in the shape of a flower, for instance, through all three layers of the quilt, then make a slit in the back, stuff extra batting into the flower shape to make it puffy, then close up the slit. In shadow trapunto the top is a piece of very thin batiste fabric, almost transparent. For stuffing you use brightly colored yarns, which take on a hazy and pastel appearance when seen through the sheer fabric.

While I love the way trapunto looks on the front of a quilt, I hate the way it looks on the back. I want my stitching to be pretty on both sides but in trapunto each hole made for inserting the stuffing has to be repaired, leaving little blobs of stitches that are not part of the design. I came up with a way to insert the stuffing from the top rather than through a hole in the back. I use a blunt tapestry needle to draw the yarn into one side of the design between the sheer top and the batting and pull it to the other side, then snip it off. The end of the thread will draw back into the design. I fill the figure one strand at a time until it is so firmly packed that it will stay in place even when I wash the quilt. It's a really slow process.

For my first trapunto work in 1985, Cindy drew out a large basket of roses for the center of the quilt with smaller designs in the corners. I stuffed each rose with bright red yarn and each leaf with an intense green that became soft, muted colors behind the sheer top. "Cindy's Rose" won best-of-show at the state fair. The crafts coordinator there asked me to send it to Disneyland in Anaheim, California, which was having an exhibit of the best quilts from all the state fairs. I did, and when I got it back, the shipping box held a best of show ribbon from Disneyland, too.

A few years later Cindy and I went to a quilt show in Tennessee and saw a quilt called "Martha's Vineyard" which had dime-sized grapes appliquéd on it. Cindy wanted me to make one, but I didn't think my appliqué skills were up to the task. I said, "Put that in a design I can do trapunto on and I'll do it, but I'm not about to do appliqué on it." A few days later she told me she had dreamed my next quilt—she keeps a pad by her bed and the night before she had sat up and sketched out the pattern.

I said "I'm ready to start it now. Draw it out for me."

She laid a piece of muslin on the bed and drew out the central figure and long triangles to indicate where the clusters of grapes would spill over the sides to the floor at the bottom corners. It took her four hours to draw it and me three years to make it. I stuffed hundreds of grapes one single strand of purple yarn at a time, then stippled large areas of the white background. Stippling involves putting thousands of stitches as close together as possible without any touching another. It gives the background a rich texture. "Cindy's Vineyard" won several awards and was exhibited at the American Folklife Festival at the Smithsonian in Washington, D.C. in 1994 and in five cities in China in 2013.

Like the grandmother in the Constitution quilt, I use a hoop rather than a quilting frame. There's not enough room in our little house to keep a frame set up, so I put one portion of the quilt in a 22-inch hoop, roll up the rest and hold it in my lap. After I put all the stitches I want in that circle, I move the hoop to another portion of the quilt and start all over again. Even when I did a king-sized quilt, I held the entire thing in my lap as I worked.

Several of my quilts were so challenging they took years to make. The most difficult one used a French technique called *broderie perse*, meaning Persian embroidery. It involved cutting floral designs out of chintz material and reassembling them into a different pattern on a quilt top. I took a piece of chintz fabric, noted the clusters of flowers on it that I wanted to use in my quilt and did a rough cut around them. To attach them to my quilt top I cut away—a half inch at a time—all the background fabric from the chintz design. I appliquéd that half-inch to the top using a button-hole stitch around the edge of each leaf, stem and flower in the design, then trimmed away another half inch of the chintz and stitched it to the piece. I kept cutting and stitching a half-inch at a time until I had a quilt top full of chintz flowers arranged the way I wanted them. It was tedious and really difficult to do. It took me five years, with R&R breaks, to finish it. When people who know anything about quilting see it they are amazed, but to most people it's just a quilt with flowers on it. Still, I'm glad I did it. It was appliqué of the highest order and got me over my fear of that technique.

Early on I learned that I could get bored or burned out working on quilts like the *broderie perse*. When that happened I'd stop and put that quilt away until I could get excited about it again. I didn't want to diminish the joy of quilting by making myself work on a difficult quilt, and when I felt that happening I would stop and do a wall hanging or a simpler piece. One of the quilts I did for rest and recreation was called the California Star or Feathered Star, but I called it my cancer recovery quilt since I worked on it during my cancer scare. It ended up on the cover of a book, *Star Quilts* by Mary Elizabeth Johnson Huff. I'm always aware that I'm uneducated and to be associated with an impressive book like that thrilled me.

White whole-cloth quilt tops make wonderful canvases for hand-stitched designs, so I've made a number of white-on-white quilts. I'm fascinated by the fact that you can take an absolutely plain white piece of fabric, sit down with a pencil, a needle, and some white thread and make something beautiful. To make one I draw the design, such as a basket of flowers, in the center of a large piece of white cloth and add smaller motifs—perhaps miniature versions of the center basket—to each corner of the quilt top. Then I fill in the background area with small designs that relate to the central one but don't take away from it—like flower buds and butterflies and feathers. I draw out every single line with a pencil; then I cover those lines with millions of hand stitches—18 to 20 per inch—each going down through the quilt top, the batting and the back of the quilt, then up to the quilt top again. The beauty of the quilt comes solely from the textures created by the stitches.

One of my white-on-white quilts won best of show at the Kentuck Crafts Festival in Northport, Alabama. That is a show with hundreds of fine artists, folk artists and craftspeople. It's an honor just to be invited, so I was flabbergasted when I got that prize, a big blue ribbon accompanied by a check for $1,000. Most awards are just ribbons or name recognition or maybe $25, so you know that Calvin and I were thrilled with that money. Then to top it off, the next year a lady from Florence, Alabama, waltzed into my booth at Kentuck and said she wanted to buy that quilt. I said, "But it's $3,000."

She said "I know. Bag it up."

I didn't know her and haven't seen her since. I think that sale shocked me more than winning best of show. It was one of the first quilts I ever sold. Most people can't or don't want to pay anything close to what a quilt is worth, so I was in the habit of keeping mine for my children and grandchildren.

Because of all the attention the *North Jefferson News* gave us when we first started the quilt guild, I became known as "the quilt lady" around Mt. Olive. Calvin had something to do with me being known outside of the community. In Birmingham there is an antebellum mansion—I think it is Birmingham's only antebellum building— which has been turned into a museum and garden. Calvin had a painting job there and struck up a friendship with the curator, Bryding Adams. He told her about my quilting, and it wasn't too long before she got a job at the Birmingham Museum of Art and looked me up. She and Gail Andrews, who is now director of the Museum, were doing a statewide quilt survey. They would go to towns in all parts of Alabama, ask people to bring in family quilts, then photograph them and collect information about the makers, the patterns, the years made, and any stories associated with them. I helped Bryding and Gail with some of those gatherings and they began to recommend me for craft shows and quilt demonstrations.

If somebody had told me 30 years ago that someday you'd be able to go outside of Berry or Mt. Olive and find people who recognized me as a quilter, I'd say "Nu-uh, there isn't a chance." But I found myself exhibiting my quilts and teaching far and wide at beautiful places like the John C. Campbell Folk School in Brasstown, North Carolina, and the Museum of Appalachia in Norris, Tennessee. This opened up a whole new world for Calvin and me. Until that time we had never been able to travel because we had a house full of kids, and even if we'd had the time, we didn't have the money. Since those who invited me usually paid most of the expenses, there was nothing to stop us. Of course Calvin would leave you with the impression that going to craft shows was not his cup of tea. He'd grumble and growl "Oh, we've got to go off this weekend. Can't do so and so," but he was always the first one ready for the trip and had more fun than anybody else on it. He would help me set up and take down my exhibit, and while I was tending to it, Calvin would be all over the festival making new friends, listening to music and thoroughly enjoying himself. ❧

> Many of the quilts described in this chapter may be seen at
> *www.outofwholecloth.com.*

In 1987 the Birmingham Museum of Art invited people who owned quilts made before 1930 to bring them to a quilt sharing day. They promoted the event with this photo of me holding a swastika quilt made in the mid-1800s by Sally Fowler. It had been left in the house deeded to Mama and Papa after they took care of Aunt Bell Fowler. The swastika, once a symbol of hospitality and friendship, was a popular quilt design until Adolph Hitler ruined it by making it the symbol of the Third Reich.

Photo courtesy of the *North Jefferson News*

Therapy

Then Calvin got sick. It started on a summer day in 1990 with what I am sure was a stroke. Calvin was planning to drive to Blount County to buy tomatoes from a farmer there. We hadn't grown any that year and I wanted some to can. Being the sociable man he was, Calvin called several people and asked them if they needed tomatoes. He planned to bring home 30 or 40 cases. That morning he felt a little dizzy but was starting to feel okay when Cindy and I left to go shopping; he said he would be leaving shortly. We returned hours later to find him down on his knees on the floor, disoriented. He hadn't been to get the tomatoes.

We tried to take him to the emergency room, but he wouldn't go nor would he go to the doctor on Monday. For three weeks after that he couldn't work because he was confused and unable to get about by himself. Even after his memory returned and he started painting again he still had times that he would get muddled. Calvin had worked in every part of Birmingham for 30-something years. He knew all the back alleys and pig trails but now he feared getting lost if he went by himself. When he needed to do errands he had to lay out the trip in a real orderly way and even then he would get confused. He quickly lost all his self-confidence.

Six months later when his hand started drawing up, he finally went to a doctor in Gardendale. That doctor diagnosed his problem as arthritis and got him an appointment with a specialist at University Hospital. If they had asked me I could have told them it wasn't arthritis—but who am I? The specialist looked at him and said, "Calvin, you are not arthritic." He made Calvin an appointment with a neurologist, who determined that he had polyneuropathy. Neither of us had ever heard of it, but the doctor explained that it is a condition that causes the nerves in your hands and feet to degenerate. It can be triggered by any number of things—infections, toxins, certain drugs, cancer, and diabetes, to name a few. The doctor said the culprit might have been a stomach virus. He said that a person could get a virus that might stay dormant for 20 years then suddenly become active and cause a painful deterioration of the nerves.

For close to six months Calvin was practically housebound. He was in excruciating pain, and the doctor switched medications back and forth to give him some relief. Some of it would make Calvin hallucinate. He'd never been on any kind of medication before, and on those drugs he didn't know if he was coming or going. Of course, he wasn't able to work. At this time he was self-employed and had no health care or disability plan. He couldn't retire and draw a pension; he simply had to stop taking jobs. He wasn't old enough to draw Social Security, so we had to wait six months until we could apply for disability benefits and another six months for the application to be approved. During that year we had no income and Calvin's medical bills were piling up. I couldn't work away from home because Calvin couldn't be left alone, so I did odd jobs, kept our grandson Brian, and sewed. But I'd go to church, and when I came out my car would be sitting full of groceries with some money to pay utility bills. People knew Calvin was sick.

During the period when he couldn't do anything or go anywhere, Calvin told Karrold, "If I ever get to the point that I can get up, I'll never sit down again."

Karrold said, "I've got a project for you," and told him about an old school bus converted into a camper that a friend of his in Warrior was selling.

"Why don't we ride up there and look at it? I think you could take it and make something out of it."

Calvin and I had always wanted something like that—a camper or a place on a lake where we could just get away. So Karrold got Calvin in the truck and took him up to Warrior to see the bus. After they looked it over Calvin called me to say he wanted it. He said they were selling it for $500 and asked me if I would help pay for it. He had started getting his disability payments and I had just gotten paid for something I'd done. He told me "If you pay $250, I'll pay

$250," and I agreed. I tell you what—when they pulled into the yard with that pathetic thing, I felt like hiding. There, taking up most of my front yard, was a motley old school bus like something from Sanford and Son. Wherever it had been repaired, it was a different color. The windows were covered in gaudy floral contact paper.

But that bus was the start of Calvin's turn-around. Even though he couldn't stand because his legs were weak and hurt so bad, there were things he could do on the bus, with help from the family. Everyday he would work on it in the front yard. When it was cold, he'd go out there with a little kerosene heater and stay as long as he could. He did a lot of the work sitting down. He started by scraping all the contact paper off with razor blades and cleaning the adhesive off with gasoline. There were already partitions in it forming a bedroom in the back, a little kitchen with a gas stove and electric refrigerator in the middle, and up front near the driver's seat was a sofa and table. It took him about a year, but with the help of Nina's husband Mark he meticulously built cabinets and added a little bathroom. Mark is a carpenter and loves a challenge better than anything. This bus was a challenge. We bought a RV commode and a good mattress and box springs for it, but otherwise we didn't have to put a lot of money into it because friends and family shared what they had. Athel Dobbs' body shop across the street furnished all the paint for the bus. We painted the exterior Chevrolet gray with black trim and painted the interior white. Karrold is a good mechanic, and he tuned up the motor for us. I made curtains.

When it was finished we took it to Fayette County and parked it by his brother Arnold's house. We tossed an extension cord out the window, ran it over to Arnold's, and plugged it in. Well, that was the grandest thing they'd seen in those parts in a long time.

The big thing to do in our family after that was to go to the country on weekends and spend the night in the bus. We loved staying under those big open skies and hearing the coyotes howl at night.

Scott would come and go hunting with his daddy as often as he could. For a while after he got sick Calvin couldn't get out in the woods to hunt anymore, so Scott shopped around for a used four-wheeler—he couldn't afford a new one—and gave him one for Christmas. The two of them would hunt, and when Scott wasn't there, Calvin hunted alone. We bought a set of walkie-talkies that had a three-mile range. He'd tell me where he was going to hunt and say, "At two o'clock I want you to turn on the walkie-talkie and check on me." We were in the country where he had grown up and knew every varmint trail in the woods. He'd walked those woods hundreds of times at night and never even needed a light, but now he didn't trust himself.

His brother Arnold was in the last stages of emphysema and Calvin felt like he needed to be in Fayette County even though he was ill. Emphysema patients tend to panic when they are by themselves, so Calvin kept him company and ran errands for his wife because she didn't drive. Their younger brother Bob, who lived half a mile away, wasn't in very good shape either. He was on disability after he injured himself by falling off a piece of machinery at the strip mine where he worked. His symptoms were a lot like Calvin's. So the two damaged brothers looked out after Arnold and pushed themselves to stay active.

It got to where we were staying in the country so much that we decided to replace the bus with a mobile home. The one we bought was almost as pitiful looking as the bus had been, but at least it wasn't in my front yard. By the time Calvin and Bob and sons and sons-in-law re-plumbed and rewired it, refinished all the walls inside, painted the outside and added a screen porch, it looked nicer than our house in Mt. Olive.

Calvin stayed there more than I did. The only way we could afford the trailer and pay off the part of Calvin's medical bills that his disability payments didn't cover was by me working. I was making wedding cakes for Nina's business and teaching quilting classes at Jeff State when I took a job doing alterations at the Bridal Boutique on the other side of Birmingham. I didn't make very much money there and I had to deal with a lot of high-strung brides, bride's maids, and mothers of brides, but each little paycheck helped us dig our way out of the hole. All of this plus the weekly quilt guild meetings and the Sunday School class I taught meant I couldn't stay in Fayette County as much as Calvin wanted me to. He was now in a period of remission where he only had to take Advil for pain, so I felt okay with the arrangement. It was difficult for him to adjust to living alone during the week, but he handled it without kicking his traces.

After Arnold died, Calvin and Bob got into gardening on a major scale. The garden came about when the Feltmans, a couple who lived near Montgomery, inherited ten acres of land close to our trailer. It had been passed down in their family for a couple of generations. They weren't ready to move there, but decided to put a mobile home on it. It was an expensive custom-built job and they decided they needed someone to watch out after it. Mr. Feltman told Calvin and Bob that if they watched the trailer, he would let them farm on his land. That suited those two brothers fine. He even bought a new Massey-Ferguson tractor so they could keep the property mowed. He didn't have the attachments, but Bob had all the plows, bush hogs, discs, and other equipment they needed. They planted beans and peas and potatoes, corn, okra, squash, tomatoes, and cucumbers and in the fall they put in rutabagas, broccoli, Brussels sprouts, cabbage, and turnip greens. Bob's mobility problems were almost as bad as Calvin's but they could do it all with the tractors. When it was time to pick vegetables, they took chairs out there. They'd pick a row and sit down, then pick another row and sit down. I honestly believe that's one of the things that helped Calvin live as long as he did; he kept pushing himself physically. He had a harder time during the winter because he couldn't tolerate the cold, but as soon as it got warm enough he was outside working in the garden and mowing grass.

Calvin had acres of grass to mow. With his riding lawn mower he tended to grass around the trailer and Arnold's house; then he'd go back to Mt. Olive and cut our grass. When that was done he'd load up the mower and go to the community center. I worried about him. After he'd leave for the center, I'd call to make sure he'd gotten there and had managed to get the mower off the truck. The community center work was all-volunteer. In the last couple of years, though, they would give him something like $20 out of petty cash to buy gas for the lawn mower since they knew we were financially strapped.

Calvin was happy to do it while he could. It was work and social time for him. If anybody he knew came down the road and saw him out there picking up litter, they'd stop and talk to him. There was a man with a vegetable stand right next to the school and Calvin would pull up beside him and visit. I told him one time they needed to buy themselves a coffee pot because all they did was sit up there and talk. But I knew that wasn't true. Calvin didn't want to waste any time. He was thankful for every moment he could be outside accomplishing something before his condition got worse.

Our children often talked about the 50th wedding anniversary party they would put on for us and there was no doubt it would be first-class since Nina was a partner in a catering company. Now we realized that the time might not come and decided to have a big do for our 45th. Naturally we had it at the community center. I did some of the cooking, but the children did all the planning and wouldn't let us near the hall on that day until shortly before our guests arrived. As expected, the girls had set it up like an elegant wedding with lace table cloths, silver serving trays, candles and flowers everywhere, a heart-shaped ice sculpture, a four-tier wedding cake, and plenty of food for our kinfolks and everyone we knew from church, the quilter's guild, the softball league, and from Mt. Olive in general.

Friends were hugging each other and chatting and ooh-and-aahing over the food and decorations when David Haynes, the editor of the *North Jefferson News*, stood up and started hushing everyone. He gave a little speech about how he'd come to know us while he was reporting on events at the community center, and when he heard about the anniversary party he wanted to contribute by making us a special video. So they turned down the lights and turned on a big TV and we all watched while photos of Calvin, the kids, and me appeared on the screen then faded into others in time to a recording of Barbra Streisand singing "The Way We Were." There were pictures of us when we were a handsome young couple followed by a snapshots of us swimming in rivers and eating at picnic tables. There was me at the barbecue grill, Calvin with the kids in their Halloween costumes, me with the girls in their Easter outfits, and another with all of us laughing because Calvin had grabbed my Easter hat and put it on his head right before the shutter clicked.

As Barbra finished her song, the opening photos of young Bettye and Calvin came up again, I guess to remind us how much had grown out of the union of two ignorant teenagers who went off to Mississippi by themselves to get married. There weren't a lot of dry eyes in the hall when the lights came up. In the video that Mark took that day, you can see Calvin furtively wipe one eye then call out to Elmer, "I was expecting them to have that one of you and me hanging like Tarzan on the grapevines."

Funerals

Back in Fayette County it seemed like the whole bunch was dying. During the years we had the trailer, we got on a first-name basis with the funeral director there. Daddy, his brother Theron, and his sister Lois all died in 1993 within four months and six days of each other. Calvin's brother Arnold died in 1994 and my mother died in 1995. Calvin's mother had Alzheimer's disease and was living with his sister, Lila.

Daddy had been disabled for the last seven or eight years with emphysema. He'd smoked heavy most of his life, but working in sawmills had a lot to do with it, too. Sawmills are the dustiest places. When it hasn't rained, a sawmill is nothing but a dust cloud. Millworkers didn't wear masks; they never heard of such things. Daddy would come in from the mill and the dust would be deep on his shoulders. You've seen pictures of coal miners when they come home from work? That's the way Daddy looked, but it was wood dust instead of coal.

When Daddy died, I thought about his disappointing qualities. He was the king of procrastination. He could care less about how the house looked. He didn't care if it was an unpainted shack and the window screens were torn and sticking out, just as long as he had some place to go to bed at night. As long as he had something to eat, he didn't care what it was. If there only was a bowl of butter beans, some cornbread, and a glass of milk on the table, that was fine with Daddy. If the roof leaked, it had to leak on him before he would repair it. I thought about how Daddy had pretty much abandoned his first children, about how he couldn't show his emotions and would walk away from his problems rather than deal with them. I thought of how he'd never accumulated any money or possessions and had little to leave his family. But I also knew he'd left us things that were worth far more than money and I decided to speak at his funeral, if they would let me.

Now Daddy didn't go to funerals. He sat outside at his parents' funerals and in the preacher's office at Doris's, but he planned his own pretty well. He'd told Clara he wanted his two nephews to conduct the service and one of his grandnieces to sing. With Clara's permission, I stood after the first preacher had spoken. I faced the family and began to talk about Daddy's talents. I told of how, without any training, he had become a first-class gunsmith, machinist, and millwright. He could make anything out of nothing. And what broke down, he could fix. I said that people in the community depended on him and respected him for his mechanical abilities. I spoke of Karrold and Milford and David, Daddy's first son by Clara, and gave examples of how they had all inherited his abilities and were using them today. I told how accomplished Doris had been, though I mainly spoke of the men in the family. The women are all capable, too, but it wouldn't work for me to talk about my talents and I didn't feel like praising Esta even though she is a masterful seamstress. Basically all I was saying was that I was thankful to Daddy for giving us good genes, because he certainly didn't nurture us. Still, it felt good to publicly say I was proud to be his daughter.

It was a different story when Mother died. It took years for me to get to the point that I even wanted to know that she was alive. Eventually, in the last years of her life, the sting was gone and I would visit her from time to time. I don't know why I did; it was more out of concern than love. Or maybe I visited because I wanted to show her that I had made it in spite of her.

She and John still lived in the two-room shanty that he had moved on to his property almost 50 years ago. At some point he set up a little barbershop beside it and he cut hair, but mainly he would sit under a shade tree. Mother, on the other hand, worked all day at one of the box or garment factories, then came home and tended her garden in the evening. She had made a very bad deal. In the last five or six years of their marriage it was obvious that she and John hated each other vehemently. One time when I was visiting he tried to get her to take her medicine. She got furious and accused him of poisoning her. She'd tried to poison my father long ago and I suppose it wasn't a stretch to suspect that someone might do the same to her.

After she was diagnosed with renal failure she needed a nursing home that offered dialysis. The only facility with an opening was in Alexander City, halfway across the state. At that point John came to court with an attorney and papers saying that he was not responsible for her so Esta was given power of attorney. She and I still felt the same way toward each other as we had as young girls washing dishes together at Mama and Papa's, and my brothers and she had butted heads over the years as well. When Esta took charge of Mother's care she told us to stay away from the nursing home. About a year later, when Mother died, Esta called Milford to give him the news and added that we were not to come to the funeral. Now she was our mother—even if she wasn't a good mother—and I didn't think one child had a right to tell the others what they could do. We all wanted the kind of closure a funeral could bring. I called the probate judge in Fayette County and he said we could go to the funeral but nothing more.

So we went. There was no visitation or wake. One of my cousins, who didn't really know her, did the service. John Hyde didn't attend, but a bunch of other kinfolks came. At the burial it was me and my family under one shade tree and Esta and her family under another shade tree. No one showed much emotion and I, for one, didn't cry. I didn't feel like I owed Mother any tears, though I was sorry that she had to die alone and unloved. The funeral for me was like closing a book. With mother and Daddy both gone, that part of my life was over.

Milford and I often talk about what we might have been if Mother and Daddy had stayed together and nurtured us. They were both smart, creative, and could do anything. When they fell apart, everything changed. Milford said he thinks about it constantly and it makes him mad as hell. Even at our age we still have hard feelings. ❧

Quilt Lady

Maybe it was a combination of the abilities I inherited from my parents and the doggedness I got from my grandmother, but somehow I did manage to amount to something—or at least the Alabama State Council on the Arts thought so. In 1995 they gave me the Alabama Folk Heritage Award, which is based on an artist's skill and knowledge of a traditional craft. I had heard of the award, but I didn't really know what an honor it was until I went to get it. The ceremony was held in an ornate, historic theater in Montgomery. People in the arts from all across the state were there to present or receive awards and others, like my family, were there to applaud the honorees. Kathryn Tucker Windham, a writer and storyteller my whole family loved, received an award that year, and Jim Nabors, who played Gomer Pyle on the Andy Griffith Show, was honored, too. Being onstage with people like that made me ask myself "What am I doing here?" It's something I doubt I'll ever forget. And of course, Calvin was in his element. He loved answering the phone when the award was announced and talking to all who called to congratulate me. At the reception after the awards program, he had big conversations with almost everyone there.

That award led to the "quilt lady" letter. There had been an article on the awards in the Sunday *Birmingham News* right on the front page of the arts section with a large color photo of me and one of my white quilts. The article told how I learned to quilt from my grandmother in Fayette County. Well, that article got picked up by one of the news services and ended up in newspapers all over the place. I know because I got letters from quilters across the country and an invitation to teach a workshop in Illinois. The most memorable letter was from a man in California who wanted to know if I was kin to Arcaster Kimbrell, a long-lost friend of his from Fayette County. He addressed his letter to

Ms. Bettye Kimbrell • "The Quilt Lady" • Berry, Alabama 35546

I'd been gone from Fayette County so long no one who worked for the post office knew Bettye Kimbrell. But instead of returning the letter, which is what any other post office would have done, they sent it out with their carriers. Each day it would go out with a different carrier who would ask folks, "Do you know Bettye Kimbrell?" Finally the letter wound up going to Flatwoods, which is down towards Tuscaloosa County, and my first cousin happened to be one of the people that the carrier asked. Wayne said, "Yes, I know who she is," and told him to take it to Calvin's brother Bob.

The gist of the letter was that the writer had seen a story about me in the *Siskiyou Daily News*. First he congratulated me on my "special gift," and then asked if I knew a Mr. Arcaster Kimbrell from Berry who had been his friend at Chillicothe Business College in Missouri 34 years ago. He was hoping I could help him get in touch with Arcaster again.

Calvin thought Arcaster was dead, but my sister-in-law said, "No, he's alive. He's in Fayette."

I said, "If he's still alive, he's in the phone book. " So I went back to the trailer and got the phone book down and there was Arcaster Kimbrell's number. I called him that night and said, "This is one of them phone calls that you're going to think is strange, but hear me out." So I read the letter to him and he was just totally delighted to hear it. The next day I took it to him and let him copy it, but I kept the original. I was floored that the Berry post office went to all that trouble to deliver it to me.

With the Heritage award came $2,500. When you live on a Social Security disability check and whatever else you can come up with, that's an awesome amount of money. It takes a lot of pressure off. I think we used it to put down a new floor in the kitchen without having to take out a loan for once. So, contrary to what Calvin had first believed, my quilting did amount to more than a hill of beans. But he already knew that. By this time he had accompanied me to so many classes and crafts shows that he knew a lot about quilting. At a show, if I had to leave my booth to go to the restroom, he could take over and answer questions about how I'd made each quilt.

He especially liked to talk about pounded leaf quilts. Some of our quilters had gone to the big quilt show in Paducah, Kentucky, that the American Quilt Society puts on each year, and they brought me back a picture of a quilt that won best of show. It was made by a woman in Westover, Alabama, who had put leaves on white fabric and pounded them with a hammer so that the chlorophyll left perfect leaf-shaped imprints on the cloth. Then she quilted on and around each leaf. At the guild that week we talked about the quilt and before long someone brought in a set of instructions for Cherokee leaf pounding from the Alabama Museum of Natural History in Moundville. So I started working on a few small pieces while we were at the trailer. I would hammer away at leaves with a small wooden mallet to transfer their shape to a scrap of fabric and then dip the fabric into a vinegar-water solution to fix the stain. The vinegar would turn the bright green stains into various shades of rusty brown. Calvin loved them.

One fall day he and Bob went out in the woods to dig ginseng. They carried all they dug to a man who was licensed to buy and re-sell it. Calvin came home pretty late in the day. He handed me a garbage bag and said, "I brought you a job." He was referring to the four wet castor bean leaves inside. Each was as big as a checker-board. He told me he'd like for me to use them on a quilt and wanted me to get out a piece of material and let him lay them out.

"I don't have enough fabric here for that." Pounded leaf quilts are made out of whole cloth, and I could tell that this one was going to take a lot of it.

"You got a truck and you know where Wal-Mart is."

The next morning I drove to Fayette and bought three yards of muslin because it was on sale. I intended to find out how big Calvin wanted his quilt and save the rest. After supper that night I told him to show me how he wanted the leaves laid out. I planned to pound them at the trailer where visitors and the telephone wouldn't bother me. He laid the leaves in a diamond pattern with their tips pointing away from each other, right in the center of all that fabric. I didn't say anything about it, figuring I would be able to cut off the excess fabric and use it for wall hangings.

We put them back in the bag where we could keep them moist and the next day I spent the whole day pounding those four leaves. I mean I pounded all . . . day . . . long. At lunch I'd eat a sandwich with one hand and pound with the other. When he came in from the garden that night I said, "OK, I've got these leaves down, now I want you to show me what you want me to cut off, because I'm going to use the rest of this fabric for something else."

He said, "No, you're not."

"If we don't cut it it's going to be so big that we'll need a lot more than four leaves on it."

"I already thought of that." He held up a pack of castor beans he had gotten from the ginseng buyer.

He said, "When I make a garden next spring I'm going to plant these and I'll grow some more." We both knew about growing castor bean bushes. Farm people planted them around their barnyards because the seeds in a castor bean are extremely toxic—in fact, they're the basis of the poison ricin—and they are known to kill moles. No farmer wants moles on his property because they dig holes that will break legs when livestock—or the farmers themselves—step in them.

He said, "Next year we can pick enough leaves to go all the way around the outside edge and you can finish the quilt."

So I took the seeds and put them in the freezer to keep them until spring, but Calvin never got to plant them. ❧

Calvin and I at the Mt. Olive Community Center in 1994.

Red Button

Before Christmas every year Cindy and Jerry would to go to Gatlinburg in the Smoky Mountains with a group of their friends. After Calvin got sick they took us instead because Cindy wanted to devote as much time to her daddy as she could while he was still able to get out. So we spent the first weekend in December there and the following week I bounced back and forth between Fayette County and Mt. Olive. It was hunting season and Calvin wanted to stay at the trailer, but I had the quilting guild to tend to, cakes to bake for Nina, a Sunday school class to teach, plus shopping and housekeeping to do and only a few brief interludes when I could stay in the country with him.

On the Sunday after our trip to the Smokies, I got a call from Calvin as soon as I got home from church. He'd broken our rake and wanted me to stop and buy another one on the way back to the trailer. He said to hurry on, though, because he wanted to go hunting a while, and he didn't want to hunt without me being nearby.

During all of this travelling, one question kept popping into my head: "What if Calvin wasn't here?" For some reason, each time I'd leave the trailer or the house in Mt. Olive, that question would well up within me. I guess I was being prepared for the fact that he was not going to be here much longer.

When I got there Sunday afternoon Calvin decided he didn't want to go hunting—he just wanted to hang around the trailer. He didn't feel bad but for some reason wanted to stay home. We carried Bob and Linda their Christmas present—a flat of pansies—then had a routine supper and were in bed by 9:00 or 9:30. Around 2 a.m. Calvin woke me up. He was in pain and wondered if he was having a heart attack. That didn't seem very likely. Calvin had participated in a couple of blood pressure studies that Kathy had gotten him into at the medical school. They'd done cardiograms and extensive tests, like one where your heart is on a monitor and you can see it—tests that would cost $5,000 if you had to pay for them. These showed that none of his arteries were blocked and both times they told Calvin something like "If the rest of you was like your heart, you'd be 18 years old."

We waited around in the trailer for a while to see if the pain would go away or get worse and then decided to drive to the hospital. There wasn't any point in calling 911. We were way out in the country and I could get him to the hospital faster than the ambulance could get to us. We grabbed his wallet with his medical cards, and headed for the truck. He told me to hurry, but to watch out for deer. "We don't need to have a wreck."

It takes about 30 minutes to drive from Berry to Fayette. As we drove into the city Calvin said, "You need to hurry." Just as I went under the traffic light at the shopping center, Calvin's head fell back and he gurgled. I reached over and shook his leg and when he didn't respond I knew that he was either unconscious or dead. I looked at the clock on the dashboard and it said 4:02.

When we got to the hospital, I was pretty sure he was dead. I sensed it by the reaction of the staff. There was immediate panic on their part. It was difficult to get Calvin out of the truck. He was a big man and getting him on that stretcher was not an easy thing, especially with the reduced staff they had at that time of the morning. When we got him on the gurney and they started into the emergency room, the woman at the desk took me aside to register Calvin. She was just absolutely flustered; when she started to ask me my name and if we had insurance, I had to calm her down before she could concentrate. I think it was the first time she had been in that situation and she could not do what she was supposed to do.

A young doctor came out of the emergency room and told the receptionist to start contacting the family. He said, "Whoever she needs, you get in touch with them," and then came to talk to me. He chose his words so carefully that they did not make sense to me. I interrupted him, saying, "I need to know what is going on here. I need you to know that I'm a Christian and I can handle the truth. I don't want hedging—no maybes and 'possiblies'. I want to know straight out what it is." He told me that Calvin was not dead, but that he had gone 45 minutes without any blood flow to the brain and if we were able to resuscitate him, there would be brain damage. He asked if I wanted to put him on life support.

I just said no. We had seen my Daddy on that machine for so long and Doris had been on it several times. Calvin had always said, "Never, never, let them do that to me." I don't think it would have worked and if it had, Calvin would have had no quality to the rest of his life. It was his time; I really think it was his time to die. Dr. Matthews said I had made a wise choice. "I'm going to go back and work with him for a few more minutes, but it looks like this is the end." He asked me if I'd called any family. "You need someone here with you."

So the receptionist started making phone calls. While I waited for Calvin's brother and our children to get there, I tried to imagine what my life was going to be like now, but there was no way to comprehend how it would be without someone I'd lived with since I was 13 years old. We had been companions most of our lives.

There was no reason for Danny to rush to Fayette from Florida, so I called him and told him that Calvin had passed and we would meet him later at home. The others did not know and they scrambled to get to the hospital to be with him. Scott received the call from the hospital and called his sisters, saying "Dad's had a heart attack and it's bad." He, Cindy, and her husband Jerry planned to drive together and Nina, who lived almost an hour south of Mt. Olive, told them she would meet them at a certain place on the highway to ride with them, then broke all the speed limits getting there. As the four of them traveled to Fayette, Scott called Danny, who said, "Just take your time and be careful driving." Scott wondered why Danny said to take your time and it didn't register until they got to the hospital. When they walked in the waiting room Scott hugged me and I said "He's gone." They met the news with total disbelief. It hadn't crossed their minds that Calvin would die. Nina went down on her knees and Cindy slid to the floor with her back against the wall. They weren't wailing or screaming, they just were overwhelmed and couldn't wrap their minds around the fact that their father was dead.

When Kathy got the call from Scott, she dressed and jumped in the car without knowing exactly how to get there. She could get to Jasper but wasn't sure how to get to Highway 102, especially in the dark. She said she just kept praying "God, I've got to find that turnoff." She ended up on a narrow slag road in a sparsely settled area. When she saw the headlights of a car about to turn onto the road, she swooped in, blocked it, jumped out, and told the men in the car "I'm trying to find highway 102. My father's had a heart attack. Can you help me? I don't know where I am." They said, "Yeah, follow us." As she did, she realized she hadn't been thinking clearly and they could be taking her anywhere. Once they reached the pavement, though, she knew where she was, passed them, tooted her horn, and was off. She arrived to find a waiting room full of family and the news that Calvin was gone.

We sat around the hospital and cried awhile, then went back to the trailer to pick up some things. I rode back with Jerry and Cindy who had left Brian in Mt. Olive with Jerry's sister, Peggy. Brian, who was eight, stayed with us every day after school, went with us on most of our quilting trips, and took part in most of our activities at the community center. He and "Peepaw" were very close. When we arrived in Mt. Olive around noon, Jerry called Peggy and asked her to bring Brian over. He said not to tell him about his grandfather; we'd tell him ourselves. I was watching out the window as Brian got out of Peggy's car. I told Cindy "He knows, because he's got Two Bear," the teddy bear he always slept with. "He wouldn't be holding on to Two Bear if he didn't know something was wrong."

Brian came inside, looked around and asked, "Where is he?" He started crying. "He's dead, isn't he?"

I said, "Yes, he's dead." Later Peggy told us about Brian's dream. He had told her "I saw Peepaw sitting on a cloud, and he had pretty white wings and he had two angels on each side and he winked at me and he spoke to me in his natural voice." He has not yet told us what Calvin said to him. I've never asked him, but I think the Lord sent Brian this dream to help him accept Calvin's death.

Putting the funeral together was hard. I had to be the strong person, because the children were on the edge of losing control. I had to sit there and not show my hurt because they were drawing their strength from me. At that point we didn't know where we were going to bury Calvin and were waiting to hear from two nearby cemeteries about available spaces. While we were at the funeral home making other arrangements, Scott's mother-in-law called us. "I want Scott to know we have sixteen plots at Oakwood Cemetery that I bought when it first opened. Y'all talk it over and if you want two of those lots, they are yours." Danny was on his way home from Florida, and we wanted to wait and talk to him before we decided definitely, but the next day we told her we would take them.

Calvin and I had discussed prearranging our funerals but had never gotten around to it. Calvin had even made an appointment with one of his friends who was part owner of a cemetery, but for some reason we had to cancel and never rescheduled. So now we had to make all sorts of decisions about who to notify, who was going to be the minister, who was going to do the music. None of us had rested well and we went through all of that operating on one cylinder.

We didn't have any life or burial insurance, so all the expenses would come out of my empty pocket. The representative who worked with us, Mr. Strickland, was aware that I didn't have money, but he knew me well enough to know I was going to pay the bill. He gave us a printed sheet that told what was required by law and what were options, and how much each costs. For instance, you could buy thank-you notes. Cindy and Scott wanted to get those but they were $75 a box so we deleted that.

Going into the casket showroom was the hardest part. We were numb, couldn't think, and were surrounded by hundreds of white coffins and gunmetal gray coffins. But one of us spied over in a corner a solid mahogany casket that looked like a piece of fine furniture. Calvin loved to work with wood. He used to refinish gunstocks for people and he made beautiful walking sticks out of trunks of young trees he found with corkscrew patterns strangled into them by vines. The coffin was lined in a slick white satin fabric that didn't seem right for Calvin, but it was the only coffin he would have picked out and we all agreed on it.

While Cindy drove me home I asked her what she thought of the casket.

"I loved it but there's only one thing that I didn't like about it—that white satin. It doesn't look like Daddy. I wish we could put a quilt inside."

As soon as we got in the door I went to my bedroom and brought out a big stack of quilts.

"Pick out the quilt you want your Daddy to be buried on and we'll take it to the funeral home."

She prowled through the quilts until she found one with a woodland scene with deer in it. It wasn't one of my major quilts; actually it was a wall hanging. I had seen the pattern in a book. It was kind of primitive looking, made from pieces of earth-tone fabrics cut in squares, triangles, and rectangles and pieced together into the shapes of deer, mountains, and trees.

"Mama, this is it. That's daddy. He was a woodsman and a deer-hunter and that's what he lived for."

It was perfect, just large enough to cover the lining that was visible in an open casket. At the visitation friends asked if we had the coffin custom-made for him.

On the day of the funeral, Mr. Strickland asked if we wanted Calvin's union pen and the quilt taken out of the casket before burial. Cindy looked at him and said, "The quilt stays. I don't want my daddy's head lying on that silk pillow." So that was Cindy's reason for burying him with a quilt, but for me it was because quilts had been such a big part of our best years together. He had helped us with the quilt guild in every way possible, and was always more proud of my quilting accomplishments and awards than I was.

When I dressed for the funeral that morning, I put on a pin that he had given me. Calvin wasn't a gift giver in the usual sense of the word, but one Christmas, five or six years past, he pulled out little boxes with gifts for the women in his life. He had struck up a friendship with a wood carver at some of the art shows we did and came home from one with four tiny hummingbird pins, hand-carved, each bird in a different stage of flight. I wore mine and when Cindy walked in, she was wearing hers. Then Kathy and Nina entered and they were wearing theirs. None of us had talked with each other about it beforehand.

My minister led the funeral service and gave the eulogy. Calvin wasn't a churchgoer, but Brother Bill and Calvin had spent a lot of time together. Years ago Brother Bill's youngest daughter had been on Calvin's ball team and in later years he often met Calvin at the community center when they were both visiting senior citizens. They had hunted together a few times and did a lot of talking, mainly about hunting dogs, since they liked the same breed. Brother Bill knew what Calvin had done in his life; he knew what was in Calvin's heart and he preached a comforting sermon that captured his personality and what he meant to people in the community. Later that week Brother Bill visited us and said he was amazed at how many people came to the funeral.

"I know I shouldn't have been surprised because of the way you and Calvin work. From where you were seated you could not see, but do you know there was not room for everybody to be seated in the chapel? We don't see that anymore in older adults. The only crowds like that are with a young person—where there's been an accident with a teenager." He said "You ought to take comfort in that."

We did, but mainly we consoled ourselves with the fact that Calvin's sudden death at the age of 62 had spared him the suffering that he was bound to face before long. That was a subject we talked about over and over again. By the time Calvin died, his right hand was pretty much non-functional and he had begun to lose the use of his left hand. He was having trouble getting about and we all knew it wouldn't be long before he was housebound. But there was a worse threat than that. His voice was sore and raspy. Calvin had smoked as long as I'd known him, and had only stopped when he got sick. I guess he'd smoked 90 per cent of his life. He was scheduled for a mandatory physical exam in January because he had changed health insurance companies, and he was sure they would tell him he had cancer. He may have been right; when Nina was taking the family floral arrangement to the funeral home, Mr. Strickland asked her how long her daddy had had cancer. I suppose morticians can recognize cancer in the bodies they are embalming.

Calvin had watched his father, his brother Arnold, Doris, and my Daddy all slowly die from emphysema and pneumonia, and early on he started talking about wanting a quick death. He had always said, "I don't want to suffer like that. I don't want to put my family through it." If he was facing emphysema or cancer I imagine he would have gone hunting and not come back. He said "I want to just go to sleep and not wake up." That's close to what happened and I think the heart attack was the Lord's way of sparing him all that agony.

In the week after the funeral we had little time to sit and cry, so we grieved as we worked. Calvin was buried on a Wednesday and the following Saturday Cindy and I headed to Fayette County to pack up our belongings. Scott, Cindy's husband Jerry, and our neighbor Rodney Dobbs came separately in a truck to pick up Calvin's four-wheeler, hunting gear, and fishing rods and reels. We weren't emotionally ready to do this but one of Calvin's kinfolks wanted to buy our mobile home and I needed all the money I could scrape up to pay the $15,000 funeral home bill.

As Cindy drove I described the night that Calvin died and all that had happened as I took him to the hospital. It was the first time I had told anyone the story. We sobbed most of the way to the trailer and continued to weep as we packed up Calvin's clothes, shoes, razor and every personal item he used in the country. At one point, Calvin's brother Bob dropped by.

"When y'all get through here, will you drop by my place? I've got something I need to tell you that I couldn't talk about at the funeral."

We promised we would, and as soon as Scott, Jerry, and Rodney left for Mt. Olive in the truck, we headed to Bob's house across the pasture from the trailer. He took us aside and proceeded to tell us something that made the hair stand up on our arms.

"On Tuesday, the day after Calvin died," he said, "I had a vision that was so clear it was like watching television. Calvin and you came into focus as you were driving to the hospital. You were going through Bankston and you asked him if he was comfortable. And before you got into Fayette, Calvin said the pain was a little more intense and to hurry and be careful."

Cindy and I looked at each other, amazed. How did he know which way I went to the hospital? There were three common routes that I could have taken and I had told no one, except Cindy that morning, which one I used. With the death Monday and all its confusion and arranging the funeral and the jillion things I had to take care of, I hadn't had a lengthy conversation with anybody. All I told the kids was I thought Calvin had died in the truck but wasn't sure until we got to the hospital.

Bob continued, "As you got into the city limits of Fayette, I saw the Lord. I could not see his face but I saw his hands and in front of him was a switchboard. And on the switchboard was a red button with Calvin's name on it and a lever. I could hear everything you and Calvin were saying, but Calvin was praying to the Lord and you didn't know he was praying. He was asking the Lord to take care of him and let him be all right. When you got to the red light at Fayette Square, the Lord spoke and said, 'Calvin, I'm going to help you, but I can't leave you there. I need you here.' He pushed the red button and Calvin's head fell back. Then he pulled down the lever and

Calvin gurgled. You grabbed his knee and shook it and then you went out of the picture and that was the last I saw. I sat straight up and looked at the clock and it was 4:02."

Somehow Bob had witnessed everything that had occurred in that trip to the hospital. There was only one thing missing from his vision. As we came to the top of the hill between Bankston and Stough, a huge buck bounded across the road. As best I could count, it had 8 points. After I had time to think about it, I wondered if it was imaginary. Usually they will stop in the middle of the road, which is why so many of them get killed. This one loped in front of us and never broke his stride. He was just there, then gone. But other than the deer, Bob got everything else right. Cindy had heard the same story twice in one day from two different people who had not talked to each other about it. She was stunned—but I understood.

God supplies us with what we need to know, not every detail we want to know, but everything we need to know to get us through. I am sure God gave Bob that dream to comfort him and let Calvin act as a witness. If Calvin could witness to only one person, Bob was a good choice. He was 20 years younger and regarded Calvin as a father figure, a mentor, the best of friends, and the closest of brothers. They had been inseparable after we set up the camper, then the mobile home, close to Bob's property. Bob had lost his oldest son to cancer, his wife was sick, and he was disabled by a mining injury. He would have been inconsolable without this revelation.

Bob told me that they had never talked about Calvin's spiritual condition. He said, "I knew he had strong convictions, but now I have no doubt where Calvin is." Bob's dream gave both of us comfort. ✺

Calvin's Quilt

This is a detail from the quilt that Calvin instigated by bringing me fresh leaves from a castor bean plant.

Calvin died December 11,1995. Christmas that year was difficult for us, but it was a healing time, too. We pretty much did what we always do. On Christmas Eve my children visit their spouses' families, so I was going to be by myself for just about the first time since the funeral. I thought I was okay with that. Cindy and Jerry dropped by briefly before they went to the Denton gathering, then I was alone. It wasn't long, though, before Nina, Mark, and their son Jake pulled up in the driveway. They had changed their plans and intended to spend the night. After they got there I was glad I didn't have to be by myself.

Of course, the whole family was there the next day to open presents and have Christmas dinner. We managed to get through the morning without breaking down until I opened my present from Scott. A couple of months earlier he had bought a set of hand-carved wind chimes for his daddy and asked me if I thought Calvin would like them. "Calvin's not the wind chime person," I said. "I'm the wind chime person." So he wrapped those wind chimes up and put them under the Christmas tree for me. I didn't know what I was opening, but when I saw them it was such a strong reminder that Calvin wasn't here that I couldn't keep myself from crying. So for a few minutes all of us were in bad shape.

After Calvin died, every time I left the house I had the urge to hurry back or call and let him know where I was. My days were full of unmet expectations. When I opened the front door I expected to see him sitting in his chair. I'd go from one room to the next and expect him to be in one of them. I'd wake up and expect him to be beside me. Pain would wash over me when I realized he wouldn't be there anymore. If Cindy and Jerry needed to go out and I was home by myself, they would come by and get me. It was either argue with them or get in the van and go.

One Sunday afternoon we were out together and it started to get dark. I said, "I'm ready to go home."

Cindy said, "Mama, Daddy's not there."

"I know, but it's a hard habit to break."

All of the children had times they missed him intensely and felt his presence. The reality of Calvin's death hit Scott when he went to Fayette County to pick up Calvin's tree stand and 4-wheeler a few days after the funeral. Scott knew how Calvin loved that 4-wheeler. It was like the good pair of feet he no longer had. Calvin had moved his tree stand to a new location he was really excited about. Scott had never seen it, but remembering his Dad's description he drove straight to it. He looked around and said to himself, "Daddy was right. This is a great spot. I don't know why I never found it." There are still times when he's hunting or working on a project that he hears Calvin's voice saying "Hey, you did a good job" or "You just screwed up big time."

On January 11, one month after Calvin died, Kathy's son Joey had his hip fused and spent 10 days at the hospital. One night after he moved into rehab, Kathy was at home asleep when her telephone rang. She panicked, thinking it had to do with Joey. She picked up the receiver and heard her dad's voice saying "Sis, how's Jo-Jo doing?" When Dennis asked what was going on she answered, "It's my Dad on the phone." Dennis said, "You've been through so much," but Kathy was sure it was a real call. Calvin was the only one who called Joey "Jo-Jo"; it was their private nickname. Kathy says she's a grounded, down-to-earth person and she knows her dad called her.

I'm not surprised that Kathy's visit from Calvin involved the telephone. He was notorious for his hovering calls to the girls after they were grown. He would call each of them every day after work. If they weren't there, he'd keep calling until he reached them and say, "What took you so long?" He wanted his children to be home and safe. Cindy remembers arriving from work and Jerry telling her "Call your daddy and tell him you made it home okay, for the love of God. He's called three times already." At times they still find themselves listening for the phone to ring as they come in the door.

He was worse after they got cell phones. He would call them as soon as they got in their cars. On rainy days he'd tell them about wrecks and what detour to take. Cindy says that when it's pouring down rain and the wipers are going wide open and she's trying to get through afternoon traffic, she'll say to herself "This is when I miss Daddy most."

Eventually the sharp pangs softened as I threw myself into making big gardens, taking care of grandchildren, quilting, and keeping the community center in one piece, but to this day I still have moments when I miss him intensely. I guess the length and depth of grief depends on the kind of relationship you had with the one who is gone. In my case, there were periods when I had as soon see Calvin going as coming, but through our 45 years together I had a steady love for him. From day one of our marriage I knew that

Calvin was the most important person in my life—even when the children came along. Now that may not be the way it's supposed to be, but that's the way I felt. I remember talking to one of Calvin's sisters about how your husband and children should rank in your relationship. I said that to me Calvin was first and the children second. She thought I was the most horrible mother there ever was for saying that. But is not that the way it should be? Eventually—if you live long enough—it goes back to that. Children marry and put their husbands and children first and you two are left with each other again.

Now that has no bearing on the way I loved my children or the way I treated them. They knew I was totally devoted to them. They also knew that whatever their Daddy wanted or needed came first. There were times he did not deserve to be treated this way and I let him know it. At such times I would tell him to walk straight or take his things somewhere else, and after a while he would walk straight. My devotion to Calvin helped him bring his life in tow and our last 15 years together were beautiful.

When I was getting ready to make my first garden without Calvin, I found those castor bean seeds I'd put in the freezer, and I planted them. Because Calvin had wanted it to be a huge quilt, I waited until the leaves were full sized, even larger than the ones he had placed on it, before I picked them. Then I pulled out the quilt top I'd started two months before he died, and pounded the leaves—ten of them— all around the border, like he wanted. The stain from the pounded leaves, after the fabric is rinsed in vinegar to preserve their color, turns greenish-brown, so I chose avocado green for my quilting thread. When I quilted around the edges of each leaf and outlined all the veins, they gained a texture that made them seem real. Then I started filling up the space between the leaves with meandering quilting stitches. Three-quarters of the way through I ran out of that particular color of thread and found out that it had been discontinued. This quilter's nightmare was over a few months later when some of the Mt. Olive quilters found a store in another state that still had it in stock. I finished "Ode to Calvin" three years after I started it. It was 110 inches square and had millions of stitches in it.

Calvin rarely complimented me on my quilts but I often heard him praise them to others at arts and crafts shows. At home if I showed him a quilt and he didn't have any negative comments about it, I knew that he liked it. This one would probably have earned his highest praise: "Yep, that's pretty good!" ✺

Laurels

Photo courtesy of Mark Gooch

This 2007 photo of me appeared in the book Carry On:
Celebrating Twenty Years of the Alabama Folk Arts
Apprenticeship Program *and was used by the National
Endowment for the Arts when I became a National
Heritage Fellow. It shows the hoop I use instead of a
quilting frame.*

Calvin's quilt went places that Calvin never got to go. It ended up
on the stage of the Strathmore Music Center in Bethesda, Maryland,
after I was named a National Heritage Fellow in 2008.

I came home after a Tuesday morning quilting session at the
community center and had a message on my machine from the Folk
and Traditional Arts division of the National Endowment for the Arts
in Washington, DC. I knew that the Alabama Folklife Association
had nominated me for an award that agency gives, so I was shaking
when I called back. I was shaking more when the director told me I
had been selected as a National Heritage Fellow. He told me it was
the highest honor given by the federal government for traditional

artists and it came with a twenty thousand dollar honorarium.

I said, "Beg your pardon—did you say t-w-e-n-t-y thousand?

"Yes, m'am, I did."

"I just wanted to make sure I was understanding correctly."

He told me the dates, September 16th through the 20th, and said someone would be in touch with me to make travel arrangements. I wondered if the government should be spending so much money on me and he told me that corporate sponsors, not taxpayers, covered all the costs.

All I could think of was how God goes before us and prepares the way. Calvin and I had no pension plan of any sort. He had belonged to the painter's union and had anticipated being able to draw from that, but there was some clause that said if you had a break in service you were ineligible and, of course, he had had some breaks. Making cakes for Nina's wedding business put a little in my pocket, but now her business was slowing down. I live off Social Security—six hundred and something a month—and can stretch that to pay Alabama Power, the phone company and the grocery store, but if I have to get a new air-conditioner, pay for a car part, get the septic tank cleaned or buy gas for a trip to a craft show, I have to do some serious figuring.

Also at the time I had been having some vision problems and didn't know how much longer I was going to be able to quilt. A few years back I had cataract surgery but it didn't help as much as we had hoped—it turned out my main problem was glaucoma. I was taking medicine for that and resting my eyes as much as I could, trying to remain an active quilter. To me the award was God's way of helping me get by and continue the work I was doing.

So on September 16, 2008, Kathy and I flew to the Baltimore Washington International Airport, where our hosts picked us up and brought us to our hotel in Bethesda. All the rest of my kids and grandkids who could get away during the week drove up together in a van to watch me be honored at all sorts of historical and prestigious sites around the Capitol. The most impressive was a banquet in the Great Hall of the Library of Congress, which is like a magnificent cathedral of books and wisdom. That night it was filled with round dining tables loaded with more silverware and crystal on both sides of the plate than I have ever seen.

The grand finale was a program featuring the 11 honorees at the Strathmore Music Center, a beautiful modern structure with 2,000 seats, most of them full that night. The honored musicians and dancers performed with their bands and dance troupes and we crafters demonstrated how we do our work, which was projected onto large screens at the sides of the stage. I, of course, showed how to pound leaves and chatted with the Master of Ceremonies about quilting while I did.

I never felt nervous at any of the events. I had made up my mind that I was the same Bettye Kimbrell in Washington, DC as I was in Mount Olive, so I wore the same dresses I wear to Mt. Olive Baptist Church every Sunday and talked about quilting at the Strathmore the same way I do at the North Jefferson Quilter's Guild every Monday night and Tuesday morning. The only time I got the jitters was when I signed the guest book at the Library of Congress. It was big and lying open and somebody was sitting there to make sure you signed it, saying "All our special guests have to sign this book." To know that my name is in it is phenomenal. Often during the trip I said to myself, "Just think . . . a needle and thread got me from Fayette County, Alabama, to the Library of Congress."

I don't think many people back in Alabama were aware of the National Heritage Fellowships or impressed that I got one, but it led to other honors for me. A producer of the awards program loved my leaf-pounded quilts and asked if I would consider donating one to be used in a travelling exhibition he was putting together. When I agreed to make him a wall-hanging, he requested that I only use kudzu leaves. Just in case you don't know, kudzu is the vine from Japan that invaded the South and smothers just about anything that folks don't tend to—hills, roadsides, even houses. I finished the piece when I got back from the ceremonies and shipped it to him. It has now been to Paris, five cities in Belgium, and will tour in the U.S. through 2015. Another of my quilts, "Cindy's Vineyard," is travelling around China in an exhibit sponsored by the United States Embassy in Beijing. Meanwhile, back home, I was featured in a documentary about Alabama crafts that still shows on Alabama Public TV from time to time.

A dream of mine came true when one of my quilts made it into the Birmingham Museum of Art in April of 2009. The exhibit featured quilts that were already in the museum's collection and none of mine were, but I guess they thought it would be good to include me because of the National Heritage award. When an assistant to the director asked me to bring my quilts down so that the people working on the exhibit could select one, I told her I would bring four since that was the most I could carry at one time across the parking lot. I was happy they selected "Ode to Calvin."

The exhibit filled two or three rooms and my quilt was the last one before the exit. When a local radio station interviewed the curator of the exhibit, she said the guards were having trouble getting people out the door because they would stop and look at it so long. They were amazed at the size of the leaves and how many stitches were in that huge quilt. If Calvin were there he would have been tickled that the wall panel misidentified the type of leaves on the quilt. I think it said they were chestnut leaves instead of castor bean leaves. He would have stayed there all day if they would let him, a big man by his big quilt, telling people that they were actually the leaves from a castor bean plant and that a ginseng buyer had given him the four in the center of the quilt and he'd grown the rest.

Calvin would have loved what happened next because of the quilt he had thought up. A gentleman saw it at the museum and contacted me about making something like it for him—just not so large. Merrill Stewart is a successful contractor of commercial buildings. When I met with him at the headquarters of Stewart Perry Construction, I could see why my work appealed to him. The offices are built on a pier over a lake surrounded by woods. Most of the walls are glass, ceiling to floor, bringing the outdoors in. The floors are made from the wood of an old tobacco barn and most of the furniture is either primitive antiques or crafted by artists that Mr. Stewart has discovered in the same way he found me.

Together we chose a size that would fit on one of the few walls that were not glass, and agreed that the design would be made with leaves from the Stewart Perry campus. One morning in July, my grandson Brian, now a college student, and I tromped through the woods across the lake and gathered morning glory vines, ferns, seven bark, hickory, oak and sassafras leaves. Over the years I've learned how to choose leaves that produce stains of varying colors. Now the leaves on my quilts tend toward soft purples, light greens or pale grays, instead of the rusty browns that my earlier ones had. All afternoon Brian and I sat beside the lake pounding the leaves into images on unbleached muslin.

I started quilting it immediately. Because of the visual problems I was experiencing, I became obsessive about finishing it before I went back for more laser treatments. I spent untold hours a day working on it and I'd go to bed at night worrying that I would go blind and wouldn't be able to finish. But I did finish it and when I delivered it, Merrill Stewart had someone from a media company there to document the unveiling.

I'm happy to say I'm not blind yet. The laser surgery and medications for my glaucoma have kept the pressure in my eyes pretty consistent in the last few years. I have been able to continue quilting by sitting in good light and taking breaks every half hour or so. In fact, after I finished that quilt, I made what is probably my best quilt ever.

Nina had been wanting me to make a leaf-pounded quilt that had a vase full of flowers as the central figure. When she found a small photograph of a two-handled Greek urn in one of her decorator magazines, she showed it to Cindy and me. We discussed how we could recreate the designs on that vase with pounded leaves and grasses. She and Cindy got together, drew the outline of the vase and penciled in its intricate figures. It was late summertime and in the neighborhood we found all the plants we needed.

For about a month we would get together as often as we could to pound leaves. This wasn't the usual work of hammering until the stain showed an entire leaf. We did that on some of the plants that were part of the arrangement in the urn, but for the decorations on the urn itself we used plant pigment to individually color all the zigzags and meanders and border designs. For instance, there was a double row of circles the size of pencil erasers that had to be hammered very carefully to stay within Cindy's pencil lines.

I refuse to keep track of how long I work on a quilt. I do not want to know. But many months later, Cindy, Nina, and I were able to admire the finished product—a large, highly decorated two-handled urn holding a loose arrangement of leaves, vines and wispy grasses arising from the center and arching over the sides. All the colors on it are soft natural ones that come from leaf pigment and all the texture comes from extensive quilting, thousands of stitches that outline the designs and wander across the background, sometimes taking the shape of hummingbirds and bees. We declared it our finest work and it was not long before Merrill Stewart added it to his collection. I have never in all my years experienced anyone who is so appreciative of the work I do. Even his grown children wrote me letters praising that quilt. ✿

This photo, made at the 2008 celebration of National Heritage Fellows in Washington, DC, was turned into a free-standing life-sized cutout which visited Paris and five cities in Belgium alongside my kudzu wall hanging.

Photograph by Alan Govenar, Courtesy Documentary Arts

Succession

The 1937 school building that became the Mt. Olive Community Center was the town's most prominent feature.

I was born in 1936. The old schoolhouse that became the Mt. Olive Community Center was built in 1937. At the time I was worrying about not being able to quilt much longer, that building was having problems with old age herself and started to need more attention than people in Mt. Olive were willing to give her. In earlier years when her wood siding started looking scabby, Calvin would set up scaffolding and some of his fellow painters would volunteer to scrape and paint the tall building inside and out. He and a few other men in the community tended to her physical ailments, but as our generation grew older and unable to do such work very few younger people were willing to step forward. Structural problems grew to a point that someone actually fell through the floor, the roof leaked like a sieve, and people complained that it was either freezing cold or boiling hot all the time. County inspectors issued reports saying it was unsafe and couldn't be repaired. The county commissioner who represented our district had long been a supporter of our seniors program and the quilt guild. She began to seek funds for a new building and worked with us to design one with rooms for meals, meetings, and entertainment for seniors; quilting frames, worktables, sewing machines and storage for the guild; and space for receptions and family reunions for the whole community.

The commissioner called me one day and said, "I've got almost enough money to start construction." I remembered another pot of money that had been saved for this purpose from the Office of Senior Citizens. It added up to the $72,000 we needed to start construction and we knew that other funds were coming that would pay for it before we moved in. We ended up with a pretty little building, sparkling clean, full of sunlight and the right size for most of our activities. For the sake of continuity the architect had specified fiber cement siding that looked like the original wood but would never need to be painted, and used doors and windows of a style similar to that of the old building. It ended up looking like a small version of the original Mt. Olive schoolhouse.

Immediately after we moved into the new building, the old one came down. As you can imagine, the demolition made people in Mt. Olive furious. There had been no hearings, no public approval process, and citizens were amazed when workers put safety fencing around the historic building and began to tear it down. I guess the county commission decided the upkeep and insurance would be too great to leave it standing, but Amy Brake, the director of the seniors program, and I got the blame. For a while I thought I was going to get tarred-and-feathered. People would come up to me in the grocery store or at church or call me on the phone and get downright ugly. I had no say in whether the building would be torn down or not, but to tell the truth, I didn't feel sad to see it go. It had been a 25-year headache. Most people didn't recognize what an effort it had been just to pay the heating and cooling bills for those big rooms with leaky windows and tall ceilings. We had told the folks in Mount Olive so many times that we needed their help, but very few responded. And of course, those who didn't were the ones who complained the loudest when it was demolished.

As time passed, public anger subsided and now people are enjoying the new building. I remain untarred. On my way to Berry I pass by a wooden schoolhouse of the old community center's era and get nostalgic, but I do not envy the people who have to keep it up.

I became president of the community center in 1976 after my predecessor died in a car accident. After 35 years I figured that I, too, would have to die to get out of office. Finally, in June of 2011 when I was nearing 74, I told the quilt guild and the center's board of directors that my health was not holding up. I had always hoped that when I got to the point I could not do a job as well as it should be done, I'd have the grace to step down. That time had come. They accepted my resignation and honored my request for no retirement parties and fanfare. Now I only go to meetings of the guild when I feel like it. It's strange to walk in, do what I want to do, and walk out without emptying the garbage can and locking the door, but I'm getting used to it.

About a year after I retired, the woman who took my place in the quilter's guild decided to step down and Kathy was elected president. She had recently retired from the University of Alabama in Birmingham, where she was an administrative supervisor in the physiology and biophysics department, and had begun working part-time at a business that does commercial quilting. She's a good hand quilter, but she also can quilt with a computerized sewing machine. I don't begrudge that.

To most quilt makers the thrill is in creating the top. Choosing fabrics, colors, and patterns and piecing them into gorgeous designs or cutting out shapes and invisibly stitching them to blocks of fabric—making decisions and revisions the whole time—that's what they enjoy most. When they put it in a frame or hoop with the back and batting and start to stitch the three parts together, however, they start to see how long that part of the process is going to take and may get overwhelmed or bored. Unless they have a group of friends to gather around a frame and stitch with them, that top may spend the rest of its life in a box in the attic since no one is shivering in the cold waiting for it to be finished. But with computerized sewing machines, you can just punch in the quilting design you want and, Lord, it just takes over and does it. And if you don't want to invest in such an expensive machine, you can take the quilt top to a quilting service like Kathy works at and get it turned into a finished quilt. With folks leading such crowded lives these days, making quilts may be a luxury that few have time for without the help of a machine.

I love hand stitching, though, and for a long time I've been on a mission to preserve it. That's why I spent so many years teaching quilting at the guild and anywhere else I was invited. And now I understand that the Internet, which for the most part I fear, can perpetuate knowledge of hand stitching even if everyone stops doing it.

The National Endowment for the Arts, Stewart Perry, and Alabama Public Television all have photos of my quilts and interviews about how to make them on their websites. When I went to the first showing of the documentary *Alabama Craft: Tradition and Innovation*, the director of Alabama Public Television told me that the film was programmed in a way that any teacher in any classroom anywhere could go online, pick that material up, and use it for instruction. He said, "Years from now when your great grandchildren are in school and want to know what you did, their teacher could pull it up in the classroom." As soon as we got to the reception, someone from the APT staff met us at the front door, grabbed my grandsons, Nick and Justin, and took them off to computers. She told them what to look for and they found it right away. Now when people ask me how to do something I can say, "Go online to the APT website and look it up." ❧

Bindings

Sometimes I think of myself 63 years ago walking up the steps of the county courthouse in Columbus, Mississippi, to marry Calvin Kimbrell. I do not see a silly 13-year-old but a young woman determined to be a good wife and raise strong children in a loving home, even if I didn't have a clue how to do it. I guess I succeeded; my children tell me they loved their childhoods. They felt our home life was stable, even though it was not, and they did not feel poor, even though we were. To accomplish that took such physical and mental stamina that I could have been totally used up by the time all five were grown. Halfway through raising my children, though, I decided I needed to nourish myself as well as my family. A blue ribbon at the State Fair showed me that quilting could be the answer. I was ready to take the basic skills my grandmother had given me and soar with them.

At one of our quilt shows years ago, the featured artist brought some of her grandmother's quilts. During a calm period on Friday I sat in the room where they were displayed and looked at the grandmother's work. I don't imagine she'd ever looked at a quilt magazine. The closest she probably ever came to seeing a printed quilt pattern would have been in a newspaper. She used feed sacks and started with traditional patterns, but each got transformed into something unique and beautiful in her hands. She was obviously an artistic person, but I doubt she would ever have gone out and bought canvas and paint. Those feed sacks were there at her fingertips, though, and she used the tools at hand—scissors, needles and thread—to express herself. All of us would like to be a Van Gogh. There is just something that God created in us that causes us to look out yonder and see, maybe, a rose blooming that's just so beautiful we want to reproduce it. I do that on muslin.

Quilting surely was part of God's plan for me. It has gotten me through some very hard times. During Calvin's drinking years I steadily quilted, one little stitch after another, with total control over the 22 inches inside the hoop I was holding, while he created all sorts of chaos. Quilting was also a means of overcoming a deep feeling of inferiority I carry with me. I grew up in a small town where everyone knew our mother had disowned us and left us to a grandmother and then a stepmother who did not want us. I am uneducated and I envy educated people. In the quilting world I've worked with a lot of folks—schoolteachers, lawyers, businesswomen, arts administrators—who have degrees. The time invariably comes when I have to fill out an application of some sort. Applications always asked what grade you finished. When I write "8th grade" and Sally over here has a PhD, it's embarrassing. To have my quilting recognized as quality art helps me feel better about myself.

And when the true Calvin came back to us, quilting was a bond between us. He suggested designs and colors for some of my quilts and helped me lug them to wherever anyone wanted me to exhibit them. Nina and Cindy have continued to help me with quilt designs and Kathy has taken over my work with the quilter's guild. Stitching has held together much more than my quilts.

Now it's time to finish my story, which is harder than finishing a quilt. The last thing I do when making one is attach a patch to the back on which I write my name and hometown and the date I finished it. Before that I have to bind or frame the edges in a way that tucks all the stuffing inside and gives the piece a finished look. When I complete the binding on a piece I've worked on for a long time and can sit back and view it as a whole, outside of the hoop and from a distance, I always feel elated. Even though I've carefully planned the design, pleasant surprises will pop out of the combination of fabrics or the types of stitches I've done. Invariably I'll also see some flaws that bother me. I've never made a quilt that didn't have a few of them, but at this point it's too late to change without ripping out a lot of stitches. On the whole, though, I usually am pleased and glad I made that quilt. That's pretty much the way I feel about my life. ✤

Bettye Kimbrell
Mount Olive, Alabama
July 2013

Publications and Websites about Bettye Kimbrell

To see color photos of quilts by Bettye Kimbrell and find topics for discussion by book groups visit: www.outofwholecloth.com

The following publications and websites provide videos and color photos of Bettye Kimbrell and her quilts, give details about specific quilting techniques and discuss the significance of her work.

Print publications

- *Carry On: Celebrating Twenty Years of the Alabama Folk Arts Apprenticeship Program.* Anne Kimzey and Joey Brackner, eds. Montgomery, AL, Alabama State Council on the Arts, 2008.

  A booklet with accompanying CD containing photos by Mark Gooch and bios of Alabama craftspersons and musicians who have served as master artists in the apprenticeship program sponsored by the Folklife Program of the Alabama State Council on the Arts.

- Mary Elizabeth Johnson Huff. *Star Quilts.* New York, NY, NTC Publishing Group, 1996.

- Paddy Bowman, Betty Carter, and Alan Governar. *Masters of Traditional Arts Education Guide.* Dallas, TX, Documentary Arts, Inc., 2011.

  This publication is an education guide with accompanying DVD describing the NEA National Heritage Fellowships 1982-2011. To order the free book and DVD, go to nea.gov/honors/heritage and click on "publications." An online version of the guide links to artist profiles and multimedia at www.mastersoftraditionalarts.org.

- *The Sum of Many Parts: 25 Quiltmakers in 21st-Century America.*
  Conceived and sponsored by the United States Embassy, Beijing,
  and developed and managed by Arts Midwest and South Arts,
  with additional assistance from the Great Lakes Quilt Center at
  Michigan State University, 2013.

  This publication serves as the program booklet for a quilt
  exhibit that took place in five cities in China, 2012 and 2013. A
  link to photos of the quilts in this exhibit may be found in tour-
  ing exhibits section of www.southarts.org.

Websites, On-line Articles, Videos, Blogs, and Podcasts

- "2008 National Heritage Fellow Bettye Kimbrell." National
  Endowment for the Arts Lifetime Honors. www.nea.gov/honors
  /heritage

  This site contains a biography, the transcription of an in-depth
  interview, and a photo of her stained-glass window quilt.

- Bettye Kimbrell interview videos. On-line educational supple-
  ment to Alabama Public Television original documentary,
  Alabama Craft: Tradition and Innovation, 2009. http://www.aptv.
  org/aptplus/digitalibrary/digitalmediashow.asp?ConceptID=15

  This site contains four videos of Bettye Kimbrell talking about
  quilting history, quilting bees, leaf pounding, and making a
  stained glass quilt.

- "Bettye Kimbrell," Wikipedia article, 2009
  http://en.wikipedia.org/wiki/Bettye_Kimbrell

- "Bettye Kimbrell Visits Stewart Perry Campus." YouTube video,
  posted by Merrill Stewart, November 4, 2009.
  http://www.youtube.com/watch?v=5PkgKfrr574

- "Bettye Kimbrell Unveils Quilt for Stewart Perry." YouTube
  video, posted by Merrill Stewart, December 10, 2009.
  http://www.youtube.com/watch?v=_8cq8KmGszg

- Beverly S. Taylor. "Bettye Kimbrell's students create lasting impressions in Cherokee leaf pounding class." *Birmingham News.* Blog. May 23, 2010.
  http://blog.al.com/living-news/2010/05/bettye_kimbrells_students_crea.html
  This blog site contains stories, photos, and a video.

- "*Masters of Traditional Arts Education Guide.*" www.mastersoftraditionalarts.org
  This is an on-line version of the printed guide listed above.

- Merrill Stewart. "Quilting to the Power of Three." Planting Acorns. Stewart Perry Company. Blog. August 8, 2013.
  http://plantingacorns.com/local-craftsmen/quilting-to-the-power-of-three/

- "Quilter Bettye Kimbrell." Alabama Arts Radio Podcast, January 23, 2011. http://alabamaartsradio.blogspot.com/2011/01/alabama-arts-radio-podcast-quilter.html
  Anne Kimzey, folklorist with the Alabama State Council on the Arts, interviews Jefferson County quilter Bettye Kimbrell about her work with 4-H Club students and their quilt exhibit at Birmingham Botanical Gardens.

- "Quilter Receives State Heritage Award." Anne Kimzey, Alabama State Council on the Arts, 1995.
  www.arts.state.al.us/actc/articles/kimbrell.htm

About the Author

Joyce H. Cauthen wrote *With Fiddle and Well-Rosined Bow: The History of Old-Time Fiddling in Alabama*, published in 1989 by the University of Alabama Press. She also produced a related recording, *Possum Up a Gum Stump: Home, Field, and Commercial Recordings of Alabama Fiddlers*, to accompany it. For the Alabama Folklife Association she edited *Benjamin Lloyd's Hymn Book: A Primitive Baptist Song Tradition* and produced an accompanying CD in 1999. Other CDs of Alabama-based music she produced include *Jesus Hits Like the Atom Bomb: John Alexander's Sterling Jubilee Singers of Bessemer* and *Bullfrog Jumped: Children's Folksongs from the Byron Arnold Collection*. She lives in Birmingham, Alabama, with her fiddle-playing husband Jim Cauthen. In their spare time they play in two old-time string bands, Red Mountain and Flying Jenny. In 2011 the Alabama State Council on the Arts honored her with a Governor's Arts Award.

About the Cover

Cindy Kimbrell Denton designed the cover and interior of *Out of Whole Cloth*. She is a professional graphic designer for Big Oak Ranch, which provides loving homes and educational opportunities for children who have been abused, abandoned or neglected. Since she was a teenager Cindy has worked closely with her mother providing drawings of designs envisioned by Bettye for her quilts. She lives in Mt. Olive, Alabama, with her husband Jerry Denton.

One of Bettye Kimbrell's white-on-white quilts serves as the background of the cover. From a flat surface stippled with thousands of minute stitches, flowers rise and become three dimensional with the use of a quilting method called traupunto. Inset on the front is a detail from one of Kimbrell's Cherokee leaf-pounding quilts. Created by staining a quilt top with the pigment of a pounded leaf and then defining its veins and edges with stitches, the piece gains additional texture from tiny meandering stitches that surround the scattered leaves. Each of the thousands of stitches in both quilts was done by hand.